PRI
THE LIONS

The untold story of the men and women who made the Lisbon Lions

DEREK NIVEN

Corkerhill Press

Published in 2017 by Corkerhill Press

Copyright © Derek Niven 2017

Derek Niven has asserted his/her right to be identified as the
author of this Work in accordance with the Copyright, Designs
and Patents Act 1988

ISBN Paperback: 978-0-9935551-2-1
ebook: 978-0-9935551-3-8

A CIP catalogue copy of this book can be
found in the British Library.

Published with the help of Indie Authors World

IndieAuthors
World

Acknowledgements

The author wishes to acknowledge the valued assistance of Indie Authors World partners Sinclair and Kim Macleod in the publishing of this book. The author also thanks his editor Gillian McGee for her usual ardent and studious efforts. A special thanks to great friends John Steele, the DJ, who always takes a keen interest in promoting my writing works, and Robin Dale, who initially encouraged me to 'kick on' with this idea. Thanks also to Bruce Bishop, a colleague and fellow published genealogical author, who has always given me cheerful and unerring advice on factual writing and publishing. As with my previous publication thanks go to the late Sir Dirk Bogarde for the pseudonym and to our old alumni Allan Glen's School for the superb education.

Finally, without the unswerving love, support and patience of my wife Linda this book would never have seen the light of day.

The young lions roar after their prey, and
seek their meat from God.
Psalms 104:21

Vene, vidi, vici (I came, I saw, I conquered)
Caesar, 47 BC to the Senate

Contents

Contents

Preface

T he casual reader may think this book is about the great game of football. On the contrary, this publication is about fate and destiny.

It examines the chance accumulation of fateful meetings and unions between men and women from the early 19th century, which culminated in the procreation of a remarkable group of young boys, who wrote themselves into the history books half a century ago. It is about men and women who were born more than 50 years before the formation of a new association football club in 1888 in the east end of Glasgow, that eventually grew into the world-renowned Glasgow Celtic Football Club. These were people who were brought together by destiny, having no idea that one day their descendants would be immortalised over a hundred years after their own births in the mid-19th century.

It could be argued that this book not only celebrates the 50th anniversary of the Lisbon Lions, but remarkably, it also marks the 130th anniversary of the club's formation. Celtic Football and Athletic Club was formally constituted at a meeting in St. Mary's Roman Catholic Church hall in East Rose Street (now Forbes Street) in the Calton, Glasgow, by Irish Marist Brother Walfrid on 6 November 1887. Its purpose was for the alleviation of poverty in the east end slums of Glasgow, by raising money for the charity Brother Walfrid had instituted, the *Poor Children's Dinner Table*.

Almost eighty years later, on a balmy evening on 25 May 1967 in the Estádio Nacional in Lisbon, Portugal, eleven young Scotsmen playing for Glasgow Celtic FC created footballing history by beating the mighty Italian side Inter Milan by 2-1 to lift the European Cup, the most prestigious club side trophy in the footballing world. They were the first British club to achieve such a feat. The legend of the Lisbon Lions was born.

Celtic remain the only Scottish club to have lifted the European Cup, but in many ways there was a unique mythical aura which emanated from this remarkable footballing feat. The Celtic team who played that evening were all local Scottish-born boys from predominantly working class backgrounds, all of whom, except one, who were born within a 12 square mile radius of Celtic Park in the east end of Glasgow. Only the forward Bobby Lennox was born 30 miles away in the coastal town of Saltcoats in Ayrshire. Another feature which the book will reveal is that 'the Bhoys' were almost exclusively products of, or came through at a young age, the dark days of the Second World War, subjected to the frightening German air raids and the hardship of rationing and post-war austerity. Whether that instilled a steely toughness which they carried on towards Lisbon is a matter of conjecture.

Looking at the exorbitantly paid international players developed nowadays at Barcelona, Real Madrid, Chelsea, Manchester United and Bayern Munich football clubs, who compete for the European Champions League, the successor to the European Cup, it can be quickly realised that never again will a team of working-class local lads ever be able to win such a coveted trophy. Billions are now spent in trying to wrest Europe's most sought after award. The legendary Celtic manager Jock Stein's only major signing in that 1966-67 season was Willie Wallace, from Hearts, to cover for the injured Joe McBride. This makes the feat achieved by the Lisbon Lions even more remarkable and unique.

In 2017 the Lisbon Lions celebrate the 50th anniversary of their landmark victory and much will be rewritten about that famous campaign of 1966-67 culminating in the final game in the Estádio Nacional. Minute detail will document the momentous game starting with Alessandro Mazzola's seventh minute penalty goal which the defensive Internazionale thought had put the game beyond the lowly Celtic's reach.

However, the Italians did not reckon on a fearsome 63rd minute strike by marauding defender Tommy Gemmell, followed twenty minutes later when, in the 83rd minute, a Bobby Murdoch shot was deftly guided into the Italian net by Stevie Chalmers to seal the victory for Celtic. All of that detail, eagerly awaited by Celtic fans around the globe, will be written, much more succinctly than myself, by authors and sports journalists who are footballing men.

The author is, instead, a professional genealogist and member of ASGRA.

The reader may ask what brought a professional genealogist to want to write the family history of the Lisbon Lions. On the evening of 25 May 1967 my mother took me, aged eleven, up to my Gran McCue's high-rise flat in Pollokshaws on the south side of Glasgow. My grandmother Annie Collie was Protestant, but my grandfather Frank McCue and his son my uncle Jim were Catholic and as my mother chatted away to her mother Annie, we 'men' sat enthralled watching the historic game unfold on the small Phillips black and white television. At the age of eleven, I was too young to go to football games on my own, so I did not immediately become a Celtic fan.

Fate lent a hand.

My father Archie was an ardent Rangers supporter and I think he wanted me to follow the Teddy Bears. To that end, on 7 September 1969, my father took me to Ibrox Park to watch Rangers face Polish side Gornik Zabrze in a UEFA Cup Winners' Cup second leg match. Rangers were trailing 3-1 from the first leg, but there was great optimism that manager Davie White's side would easily overcome that score in the return match on home turf. That optimism was totally dispelled that damp evening when Rangers were beaten by another 3-1, going down 6-2 to Gornik. The defeat ended Davie White's managerial career, but as my father and I trudged despondently back from Ibrox Park to Corkerhill, Archie uttered these fateful words, "I'll never be back at Ibrox again." Although I have a copy of the match programme, given to me on my retirement from the rail industry in 2007 by my great railway colleague, DJ Steeley, it seems to serve as a reminder of my father's dismissive words and that Rangers was not the team for me at that point in my young life.

Celtic at that time continued to be in the ascendency in Scottish football. They were on course for a new record-breaking 'nine-in-a-row' league championship titles and another final appearance in the European Cup against the Dutch team Feyenoord in 1970. I decided that Celtic was the team I wanted to support. My father, although a Protestant, had no objections, although probably deep down he would rather have seen me go to Ibrox. Two of my younger brothers, James and David, went on to become ardent Rangers supporters.

By the time I was taken to Parkhead for the first time in the 1970-71 season my family had moved to the sprawling suburban housing estate of Pollok. I travelled on the Pollok Celtic Supporter's Club bus accompanied by my upstairs neighbour John Dillon, a life-long Celtic fan. Thereafter, I would go along to Parkhead as often as I could afford to support the Hoops. Things began to change when I joined British Rail in August 1973 at their Scottish HQ building in Port Dundas, Cowcaddens, Glasgow.

I soon found a different atmosphere in Buchanan House to the one at home where my father was indifferent to my choice of team. Although my parents were from a 'mixed marriage' religion or bigotry was never a feature in our home. In the claustrophobia of an office atmosphere there were clear dividing lines, where Protestants supported Rangers and Catholics supported Celtic. It was a complete anathema to have a young Protestant supporting Celtic and this was made quite clear to me in no uncertain terms.

This was also set against a background whereby 'The Troubles' had exploded violently in Northern Ireland and sectarian divisions were also crystallised in Glasgow and the west of Scotland. The British Rail HQ at Buchanan House where I worked could be evacuated two or three times a week with hoax bomb scares. There was an increasing section of the Celtic support who were showing allegiance to the nationalist cause in Northern Ireland, mainly displayed through sectarian singing and provocative banners. By the autumn of

1974, I was finding it more difficult to reconcile my support to Celtic, with the jibes I had to face at work and the growing menacing atmosphere that I felt standing in the Jungle at Parkhead.

I remember vividly going to a midweek evening cup tie at Fir Park where Celtic were playing Motherwell. I cannot recall the score, but my recollection is that the game was not going well for Celtic and the atmosphere was becoming positively acerbic. The Celtic fans were jam-packed into the stand opposite the Motherwell main stand and the next thing I remember was the young girl standing next to me collapsing after being hit by a bottle half-filled with goodness knows what. She had to be stretchered away by the St Andrew's Ambulance and we spent the rest of the game watching our backs more than what was happening on the pitch.

I only ever attended one Old Firm match. I had been asked by my brother-in-law Ronnie, an avid Rangers fan, if we could go together and naïvely I agreed. We both paid to get in at the Celtic end and Ronnie joked that he hoped that Rangers would not score as he might accidentally reveal his true colours in a sea of green and white. For anyone who has never attended an Old Firm match it is difficult to describe the atmosphere. I can only describe it akin to two warring enemy armies standing facing each other on a blood-soaked battlefield. I am sure that many Rangers and Celtic fans love the atmosphere, but I felt distinctly uncomfortable that day.

Even more so with my Rangers loving brother-in-law standing beside me. Celtic scored first and it was quite amusing to watch Ronnie, showing no trace of emotion, being hugged generously by the surrounding Celtic fans. In the second half Rangers forced an equaliser and it was just as amusing to see Ronnie standing alongside all the disconsolate Hoops fans and not twitching a muscle. I am sure his hands were doing cartwheels in his pockets. Fortunately, the game ended 1-1 which took the sting out of the bilious atmosphere and Ronnie and I got out of Parkhead alive.

Old Firm fans will be well aware that sectarian hatred transcends even those titanic battles which perennially take place at Parkhead and Ibrox. When my daughter was very young I got the chance on a couple of occasions for two free exclusive main stand tickets at Ibrox. I well remember a game, I believe around 1994, where Rangers were playing Motherwell at home and we were sitting only a few rows down from the Director's Box and just behind two very smartly dressed elderly gentlemen. The two elderly Rangers supporters commented on my daughter's young age, how pretty she looked and how great it was to see such a young new supporter.

As the game got underway Motherwell were actually playing extremely solidly at the back and attacking well on the break. The two elderly gents were getting more agitated at Rangers' failure to contain the 'Well. From memory, I believe it was the late great Phil O'Donnell, prior to his time at Parkhead, who picked up the ball on the halfway line just under us sitting in the main stand. As he surged forward one of the old gents screamed out at the Rangers defence, "Break that Fenian b*****d's leg!" Suffice to say that was the last time I took my daughter to a game of football in the west of Scotland.

The last game I remember going to at Celtic Park was on

the evening of 10 April 1974. It had been pouring heavily all evening and when my old railway boss John Campbell, also a big Hoops fan, and I arrived at Parkhead for the European Cup semi-final first leg game against Spanish side Atletico Madrid the queues were enormous. That crushing trip to the turnstiles was scary in itself, dragged through huge puddles up to our ankles. In fact, at one point the crush was so bad that all of a sudden I was pinned in by so many bodies and my feet were not touching the ground.

The game had actually kicked off by the time John and I got into the ground. When we finally arrived in the Jungle stand, John and I thought that we were fortunate not to have missed all the goals Celtic were going to knock in that evening. However, in the end it could not be classed as a game of football. The ultra-defensively minded Atletico side kicked the poor Celtic players off the park that night and although the Spaniards had three men sent off for violent conduct, they still managed to hold out for a 0-0 draw. Poor wee Jimmy Johnstone was photographed in the press the following day with his legs covered in cuts and bruises. Atletico won 1-0 in the return leg in Madrid. Celtic were out of the European Cup and my interests turned away from going to support Celtic.

However, it was that support for Celtic dating back to 1967 that kindled within my soul this book idea.

The book sets out to celebrate the 50th anniversary of the Lisbon Lions not from a footballing perspective but from a genealogical, familial, religious and social history perspective. It sets out to tell the story of the Lisbon Lions from the viewpoint of the people who made that unique group of players, i.e., the direct ancestors of the Lions, from the point of view of their origins, lives, loves and occupations. This book will also demonstrate through the ancestry of the Lisbon Lions that they were all from different sects of the Christian faith and that the Protestant/Catholic divide that persists in the west of Scotland was meaningless to their quest for success. Jock Stein was once asked why he seemed to be signing too many Protestants for Celtic. Stein joked that he was signing up all the good Protestant ball players to ensure they did not end up at Ibrox, because he knew Rangers would not sign any good Catholic players at that time.

Although, the legend persists of a small group of local boys born within a 30 square mile radius, the book will demonstrate a varied ancestry which spreads their family history over a much wider global net. The story will take the reader on a journey back throughout much of Scotland, into Ireland and beyond the British Isles, believe it or not, to countries in Eastern Europe. Ironically, no English ancestry emerged in any of the players' family trees and these were players who loved to beat English opposition at club and national level.

The narrative will throw up some controversy among Celtic aficionados due to my decision on who to include, or not include, as 'Lisbon Lions' for the content of this book. Some Celtic fans will be horrified to note that the management team will not be included in this book, but that should not detract from the incredible achievements of the legendary manager Jock Stein, assistant manager Sean Fallon and trainer coach Neil Mochan, who also received winners medals in 1967.

In fact, Stein's achievements as a manager are so monumental that he would deserve a book in his own rights. However, when most Celtic fans think back fondly on the Lisbon Lions,

I feel sure that their memories are for the players, and if asked they could rhyme the winning team off like some favourite song: Simpson, Craig, Gemmell, Murdoch, McNeill, Clark, Johnstone, Wallace, Chalmers, Auld and Lennox. Those were the names of the legendary 11 players who beat Inter Milan 2-1 on 25 May 1967.

However, again this book will continue to be controversial, in that the book will outline the ancestry of all 16 players who played their part in the 1966-67 campaign and were awarded winners medals. It is reckoned that Jock Stein personally wrote to UEFA to ensure that all 16 players were recognised.

This included the substitute goalkeeper John Fallon who was on the bench in Lisbon, but who was not used by Stein in the game. In fact, so defensive were Inter that goalkeeper Ronnie Simpson hardly broke sweat himself in the game. Also recognised as winners were Joe McBride and John 'Yogi' Hughes, both of whom were out injured for the final, Willie O'Neill and Charlie Gallagher; all four having made appearances throughout the 1966-67 European Cup campaign. For that reason the Lisbon Lions, for the purposes of this book, will be all of the 16 players who rightly and proudly lifted winners' medals for the 1967 European Cup campaign.

This book serves to show that even in greatness we are, as we say in Scotland, "a' Jock Tamson's bairns". My own family history is a tale of poor, struggling agricultural labourers, coal miners and railway workers striving to achieve more than their working class existences afforded them. Within my own history are stories of heroism through two great wars, tales of illegitimacy, infant mortality, the poorhouse and grinding poverty. The average reader will be able to associate their family history in the same vein.

Likewise, the genealogy of the Lisbon Lions reveals a remarkably similar story of ordinary working class boys from predominantly poor backgrounds who went on to achieve something extraordinary. The reader should be aware that it has not been possible to research every aspect of the lives of the ancestors of the Lions and in the main the detailed research concentrates on the Bhoys' Scottish family history. Also, many of the Bhoys have now passed on to that great Paradise in the firmament. In fact, Lion Tommy Gemmell sadly passed away as the book was being finalised, but the book will not discuss their passing. Thus, the Lisbon Lions will remain immortal, even within the confines of this book.

The Lisbon Lions.

This is their amazing history.

Part 1

The Lisbon Lions Players
25 May 1967

Estádio Nacional, Lisbon, Portugal

Chapter 1

Ronnie Simpson (Goalkeeper)

Honours as a Celtic player:
1 European Cup
4 Scottish League titles
3 Scottish Cups
5 Scottish League Cups
Scottish Footballer of the Year 1967
(aged 36)

The young Ronnie Simpson

Ronnie Simpson, nicknamed 'Faither' by his team mates, was by far the oldest of the Lisbon Lions. Ronnie was more than 10 years older than some of the younger players. Ronald Campbell Simpson was born on 11 October 1930 at 197 Kingsacre Road, Kings Park, Glasgow, in the recently built cottage flats, virtually in the shadow of Scotland's national stadium Hampden Park, where Ronnie would play some of his finest games for Celtic and Scotland. Although Ronnie was born against the backdrop of the Great Depression, his family were, to some extent, cocooned from its terrible economic and social effects. Kings Park at that time was one of the new affluent garden suburbs being constructed in the outskirts of Glasgow for those who still had money in their pockets.

Ronnie's father was James McMillan Simpson, a professional football player, and his mother was Mabel Norma Samson Campbell. It will not be widely known to many Celtic supporters nowadays that Jimmy Simpson was, at the time of Ronnie's birth, playing centre half for - and would later become captain of - Glasgow Rangers, Celtic's long time arch-rivals. Who would have guessed that the son of a Ranger's captain would go on to become one of the immortal Lions?

Ronnie started his senior career with amateur club Queen's Park at Hampden Park near his family home. Ronnie was selected by their first team in 1945, aged just 14 years and 304 days, which was an unofficial Scottish record, due to the suspension of normal competitive football during World War II. He attended Kings Park Secondary School and was playing in goal regularly every Saturday morning for the school team. One Friday afternoon in June 1945, Ronnie was solemnly dispatched by his teacher to the headmaster's office, assuming that he was in for the belt. However, the headmaster Mr Hodge had two auspicious visitors. They were scouts from Queens Park FC, the local team that Ronnie had supported as a boy. They had come to request whether Ronnie was free to play at Hampden Park on the following day – Saturday. Ronnie later wrote that he could not believe what he was hearing.

Queens Park were playing a second leg tie against the 'Bully Wee' Clyde in the Summer Cup and their regular goalkeeper Bobby Brown, who later became Scotland manager, was serving his country in the Royal Navy. Ronnie was keen to play, but he suggested the Queens Park scouts speak to his father Jimmy, who would be returning home on leave that evening.

Jimmy Simpson was serving in the RAF and he had been stationed in Stoke at that time. It was after 11pm before Jimmy got home but he immediately agreed to let Ronnie play for Queens Park. Young Ronnie could not believe that he would be stepping into the boots of his great idol Bobby Brown.

Ironically, Mr Hodge, who was himself a Queens Park supporter and whose son Lindsay Hodge played outside-right for, still insisted that Ronnie played in the Saturday morning game for Kings Park before reporting to Hampden Park for the First Division game. Queens Park won 5-2 on aggregate over Clyde and Ronnie had been victorious in his first senior game. The press headlined him as 'The Schoolboy Hampden Hero'. Ronnie was signed on as a Queens Park goalkeeper, as an understudy to Bobby Brown and his senior footballing career had begun, although he stayed on at school for a further year.

Simpson also represented the Scotland Youth side in a match against England Youth played on 25 October 1947 at Belle Vue, Doncaster. He was selected by the legendary manager Matt Busby to play for the Great Britain squad in the 1948 Summer Olympics in London. Simpson's performances earned him a trial with his father Jimmy's old club Glasgow Rangers, but, the Ibrox club did not sign him. Following his National Service between 1948 and 1950 Ronnie moved to the now defunct Third Lanark at Cathkin Park.

Ronnie then spent nine years at Newcastle United winning the FA Cup twice in 1952 and 1955 for the St James's Park outfit. In 1960 Simpson signed for Hibernian and helped to save them from relegation in 1962. However, he fell out with the then young manager Jock Stein over Simpson's attitude to training and Stein sold him to Celtic in 1964. Celtic had signed him as cover for their young goalkeeper John Fallon and when Jock Stein joined Celtic as manager later in the 1964-65 season it was thought Simpson would make a sharp exit from Parkhead. However, after Fallon took the brunt of criticism for Celtic's defeat to Rangers in the 1964 Scottish Cup final, Simpson became Stein's first choice goalkeeper. Ronnie's path of destiny towards Lisbon was now set.

In that amazing year for 'Faither', Ronnie Simpson also won his first full cap for Scotland in 1967 in the famous 3-2 victory at Wembley over England, who had been crowned World Champions in 1966. Also in the fabled side that day was his Lions teammates Tommy Gemmell, Willie Wallace and Bobby Lennox, the game being dictated by Rangers' Jim Baxter in midfield, who cheekily played keepie-up, and Manchester United's Denis Law up front. Ronnie's father Jimmy was in the crowd that sunny day at Wembley, as was the author's own father Archie, a locomotive driver at Cork-erhill Depot, who had travelled down with his driver mate John Murdoch on a supporters' special on their free British Railway staff passes. My father Archie and his pal Murdoch, no relation to Bobby, were great Rangers supporters.

Ronnie's parents -James McMillan Simpson and Mabel Norma Samson Campbell

Ronnie's father James McMillan Simpson was born out of wedlock on 29 October 1908 at Melville Road, Ladybank, Fife to father Alexander Simpson, a ploughman, and mother Annie McMillan Howatson. The birth was registered by his mother Annie M Howatson and his father Alexander Simpson, who was living at Kilmaron Farm, Cupar at that time, on 14 November 1908 at the Ladybank Registry Office. However, in a Register of Corrected Entries for the parish of Collessie in Fife, James's birth was 'legitimated by the subsequent marriage of its parents – such marriage being registered in this parish, dated 30 April 1910'.

By the time Jimmy was two his father Alexander was working as a police constable in Dundee. In 1911 census James, age 2, resided at 3 Canning Street, St Paul, Dundee with his father Alex Simpson, 22, a police constable, and mother Annie, 25. As Jimmy grew up he showed great promise as a footballer and his ambition as a young boy in Dundee was to play professional football.

Jimmy, aged 16, achieved this ambition and he signed for Dundee United in 1924 and made his playing debut at the age of 17 as a wing half. Jimmy was a regular during the club's first two years in the Scottish League Division One, however, United could not retain him following his team's relegation in 1927. The young Jimmy was transferred to the Glasgow Rangers for the then substantial signing on fee of £1,000. At Ibrox Stadium he was converted into playing as a centre half and he became an integral part of the team which dominated the Scottish game during the 1930s.

Jimmy won five League championships and four Scottish Cups, adding four Scottish League caps and 14 full Scottish international caps to his collection. During WWII Jimmy enlisted in the RAF, being mainly based at Stoke in Staffordshire. One Friday in June 1945, following VE Day, Jimmy returned home on leave to Kings Park to find his son Ronnie eagerly awaiting his father's arrival. Jimmy agreed with the scouts from Queens Park to allow his 14 year old son to play for them the next day against Clyde.

In 1945, during his RAF service Jimmy still managed to play as much football as he could; guesting for St Mirren, Dundee United and Stoke City. He also played a great deal for the RAF Select teams. After being de-mobbed Jimmy Simpson returned to Ibrox Park. He left Rangers in July 1946 to take up a player–coach role with Highland League club Buckie Thistle. Jimmy was then appointed as manager of Alloa Athletic on 19 December 1947, but he left the club by mutual agreement on 19 February 1949. He had served an impressive career as a professional player as centre-half and captain of both Rangers and Scotland.

Ronnie's mother Mabel Norma Samson Campbell was born on 11 December 1907 at 27 Clepington Street, St Andrew, Dundee to father Robert Clark Campbell, a railway signal-man, and mother Lily Samson. The birth was registered by Mabel's father Robert on 30 December 1907 at the Dundee Registry Office. After leaving school Mabel worked as a sack machinist, most likely in one of Dundee's many jute factories. The manufacturing of jute and its products was the staple industry of Dundee at that time.

James McMillan Simpson, 20, a professional footballer, of 3 Canning Street, Dundee married wife Mabel Norma Samson Campbell, 21, a sack machinist, residing at 19 Clepington Street, Dundee on 18 July 1929 at the Regent Restaurant, Nethergate, Dundee according to the forms of the Church of Scotland. The wedding was conducted by Rev David Dick, minister of Clepington Church; the best man was Thomas Batchelor, of 11 High Street, Newburgh and the best maid was Alexandra Campbell, Mabel's sister, of West Haven, Carnoustie.

By the time Jimmy and Mabel's son Ronnie was born in 1930, Jimmy was a firm favourite in the Rangers' first team and he had bought one of the new cottage flats in Kings Park, Glasgow. Jimmy and Mabel's son Ronald Campbell Simpson was born on 11 October 1930 at 197 Kingsacre Road, Kings Park, Glasgow. The birth was registered by father James on 22 October 1930 at the Glasgow Registry Office.

Later, Jimmy also qualified as an engineer, which became his main occupation after he had retired from football. However, his proudest moments must have come in that monumental year of 1967, watching his son Ronnie lift the European Cup and then for Ronnie to go on to win his first cap for Scotland against great rivals England in the 3-2 victory with the 'Wembley Wizards'.

James McMillan Simpson, 63, a barman, died on 27 May 1972 at 197 Kingsacre Road, Kings Park, Glasgow as registered by his son Ronnie. Ronnie's mother Mabel was still alive in 1972 after the death of her husband Jimmy and she continued to live at their home in Kings Park.

Ronnie's paternal grandparents – Alexander Simpson and Annie McMillan Howatson

Alexander Simpson, aka Alex, was born on 6 February 1889 at Springfield, Cupar, Fife to father James Annan Simpson, a carter, and mother Elizabeth Jane Robertson. The birth was registered by Alexander's father James on 13 February 1889 at the Cupar Registry Office. Alexander grew up in the landward village of Springfield, Cupar and in 1901 census Alexander, 12, a scholar, was residing there with his grandmother Euphemia Simpson, 78, a widowed grocer. After schooling Alex became a farm servant and then a ploughman at Kilmaron Farm in Cupar.

Annie McMillan Howatson was born around 1886 in Colmonell, Ayrshire to father William Howatson, a dairyman, and mother Grace McCracken. After Annie left school she trained to become a dressmaker. Alexander and Annie met and fell in love and Annie soon fell pregnant with their son James. Their son James McMillan Simpson was born out of wedlock on 29 October 1908 at Melville Road, Ladybank, Fife. The birth was registered by his mother Annie M Howatson and his father Alexander Simpson, who was living at Kilmaron Farm, Cupar at that time, on 14 November 1908 at the Ladybank Registry Office. However, in a Register of Corrected Entries for the parish of Collessie in Fife, James's birth was 'legitimated by the subsequent marriage of its parents – such marriage being registered in this parish, dated 30 April 1910'.

Alexander, who was by then working as a police constable in Dundee, and Annie had married the previous day. Alexander Simpson, 21, a police constable, residing at 109 Strathmartine Road, Dundee married wife Annie McMillan Howatson, 24, a dressmaker, residing at Melville Road, Ladybank, Fife on 29 April 1910 at Annie's home according to the forms of the Church of Scotland. The wedding was conducted by Rev Robert Taggart Kerr; the best man was William Robertson and the best maid was Polly Howatson, Annie's sister.

In 1911 census Alex, 22, a police constable, resided at 3

Canning Street, St Paul, Dundee with wife Annie, 25, and son James, 2. Alexander and Annie were both still alive in 1929 and saw their son James sign professionally for Dundee United and Glasgow Rangers. After Annie's death Alex Simpson, by then a police sergeant, married his second wife Jane Hunter. Alexander Simpson, 77, a retired police sergeant, died on 23 June 1966 at Ash Villa, Kingskettle in Fife. He had not lived long enough to see his grandson Ronnie Simpson's greatest achievement in Lisbon - just 11 months later.

Ronnie's maternal grandparents – Robert Campbell and Lily Samson

Robert Campbell and Lily Samson were born around 1880 and they were married on 21 June 1907 in the village of Panbride, near Carnoustie, in Forfarshire, now in the county of Angus. Later that same year Robert was working as a railway signalman in Dundee, most likely with the North British Railway Company. Dundee was one of the great railway hubs in Scotland at that time, with trains coming to and from Glasgow via Perth, Edinburgh via Kirkcaldy; also from England via the East Coast Main Line and going to and from the north to Aberdeen and Inverness via Elgin.

Robert would only have been a glimmer in his mother's eye, when, 18 years previously, Dundee was struck by disaster. On 28 December 1879 the original Tay Railway Bridge collapsed during a violent storm sweeping a loaded train into the icy waters killing ninety passengers and crew. The disaster was eulogised by Scotland's 'worst ever poet' William Topaz McGonagall. No-one survived, however, the steam engine hauling the train was recovered from the River Tay and when Robert Campbell was working as a railway signalman in 1907, the engine - nicknamed 'The Diver' - was still hauling trains through Dundee for the North British Railway.

Robert and Lily had two known daughters; Mabel and Alexandra. Their daughter Mabel Norma Samson Campbell was born at 11.35pm on 11 December 1907 at 27 Clepington Street, St Andrew, Dundee. The birth was registered by Mabel's father Robert Clark Campbell on 30 December 1907 at the Dundee Registry Office. Clepington Street is just off Tannadice Street, which is a stone's throw from Dundee United's football ground, where Robert and Lily's son-in-law Jimmy Simpson started his professional football career. Robert and Lily were still alive in 1929 when Jimmy was playing at Tannadice.

Ronnie's great-grandparents

On Ronnie's paternal line was his great-grandfather James Annan Simpson and his great-grandmother Elizabeth Jane Robertson, aka Elizabeth Imrie Robertson. James was born on 10 May 1861 at Pitscottie Mill, Ceres, Fife to father Alexander Simpson, a mill worker, and mother Euphemia Henderson aka Elspet. Elizabeth was born around 1867 to father William Robertson, a farmer, and mother Janet Davidson. In 1871 census James, age 9, a scholar resided with his parents Alex and Euphemia and his siblings at Mill Hall, Ferry Port on Craig, Fife.

James Annan Simpson, 27, a coachman, married wife Elizabeth Jane Robertson, 21, a domestic servant, both residing at

Russell Mill, Springfield, Cupar on 23 November 1888 at Park Avenue Hall, Dundee according to the forms of the Church of Scotland. The wedding was conducted by Rev James M Campbell, minister of Wallacetown, Dundee; the best man was Alex Shaw and the best maid was Mary R Davidson. James and Elizabeth would have been completely oblivious to the fact that just six months prior to their marriage the newly constituted Glasgow Celtic Football Club played its first match on 28 May 1888. Celtic played a friendly match against, what would become their greatest rivals, Rangers and the east end team won 5-2.

Their son Alexander Simpson was born on 6 February 1889 at Springfield, Cupar, Fife. The birth was registered by Alexander's father James on 13 February 1889 at the Cupar Registry Office. A few months later in 1889 Celtic reached the final of the Scottish Cup for the first time, only to lose 2-1.

James, by then working as a ploughman, and Elizabeth were both still alive in 1910 when their son Alexander Simpson married wife Annie Howatson. James Annan Simpson lived to see his grandson James McMillan Simpson sign as a professional footballer for Dundee United in 1924, although he was dead before young James went on to greater things with Rangers and Scotland. James Annan Simpson, a farm servant, married to Elizabeth Robertson, died on 26 March 1925 at Easter Kilmany, Kilmany, Fife as registered by his son Alexander Simpson of 3 Canning Street, Dundee. Elizabeth Imrie Robertson was recorded as dead before 1966 by her grandson R A Simpson, Jimmy Simpson's brother.

On Ronnie's paternal side was his other great-grandfather William Howatson, a dairyman, and his great-grandmother

Grace McCracken. They had two known daughters; Annie McMillan Howatson (b. ~1886) in Colmonell, Ayrshire and Polly. William Howatson, a dairyman, was dead by 1910 and his wife Grace was a widow when her daughter Annie married Alexander Simpson.

Ronnie's great-great-grandparents

On Ronnie's paternal line was his great-great-grandfather Alexander Simpson and his great-great-grandmother Euphemia Henderson. Alexander Simpson, aka Alex, was born around 1817 in the parish of Ceres, Fife. Alex grew up to be a farm labourer and later on a mill worker. Euphemia Henderson, aka Elspet, was born around 1822 also in Ceres, Fife. Alex Simpson married wife Euphemia Henderson on the 18 February 1844 in Kemback parish as recorded in the Old Parish Records as follows:-

> *OPR Marriages Kemback 433/2: 1844: Alex Simpson in the parish of Ceres & Elspet Henderson in this parish were proclaimed Feb[ruary] 18 1844*

Alex and Euphemia had seven known children; Elspet, Robert, John, James, Jean, Elizabeth and Agnes. In 1851 census Alex Simpson, 34, a farm labourer, resided at Bothy of Drumcarro, Cameron, Fife with wife Euphemia, 29, children Elspet, 4, Robert, 2, and baby John, only 2 months old. Ten years later, son James Annan Simpson was born on 10 May 1861 at Pitscottie Mill, Ceres, Fife to father Alexander Simpson, a mill worker, and mother Euphemia Henderson.

In 1871 census Alex Simpson, 53, a labourer, resided at Mill Hall, Ferry Port on Craig, Fife with wife Euphemia, 48,

Robert, 22, a mechanic, John, 20, a flax dresser, James, 9, a scholar, Jean, 25, a mill worker, Elizabeth, 14, a mill worker, and Agnes, 13, a mill worker. Also residing at Alex's home was a lodger Mary Henderson, 50, a mill worker, and likely to be Euphemia's unmarried sister. Alex, a stoker in a factory, was recorded as dead by 1888.

By 1901 Euphemia his widow was running a grocer's shop in Springfield, Cupar in Fife. In 1901 census Euphemia Simpson, 78, a widowed grocer, resided in Springfield, Cupar with her widowed daughter Jean Greig, 55, a jute reeler, and five grandchildren including Alexander Simpson, 12, a scholar. Euphemia Simpson was dead before 1925.

Still on the paternal line was Ronnie's other great-great-grandfather William Robertson, a farmer, and his great-great-grandmother Janet Davidson. William and Janet had a daughter Elizabeth Jane (or Imrie) Robertson born around 1867. William Robertson, a farmer, was dead by 1888 and his wife Janet was a widow by then.

Chapter 2

Jim Craig (right back)

Honours as a Celtic player:

1 European Cup

7 Scottish League titles

4 Scottish Cups

4 Scottish League Cups

The young Jim Craig

Jim Craig was out of a slightly different mould from the other Lions, who could all affirm that they came from poor working class backgrounds. Jim was privileged enough to be able to attend Glasgow University to study for a degree in dentistry and after retiring from football he ran a successful dental practice in Glasgow. James Philip Craig was born on 30 April 1943, during WWII, at his grandparents' home at 222 Drumoyne Road, Govan, Glasgow to father James Forbes McIntyre Craig, a drapery salesman, and mother Margaret Hughes. The birth was registered by Jim's father James F Craig on 1 May 1943 at the Glasgow Registry Office. At the time of Jim's birth his father James was still fighting for his country as a seaman in the Royal Navy.

Jim was born within the shadow of Ibrox Park in Govan but his heart was set on playing for their great rivals in the east end of Glasgow. Although his parents were raised in mixed religions, Jim was raised in the Roman Catholic faith. Jim was a Celtic Bhoy through and through and he is recognised an aficionado on the history of the club.

After his schooling Jim was signed on amateur terms under then manager Jimmy McGrory at Celtic, but he was determined to continue with his dental degree at Glasgow University. Jim played regularly for the university first XI and his earliest significant match was playing for the Scotland universities side against the 'Auld Enemy' England. Jim gained his degree in dentistry, however, he continued to progress well at Celtic and he signed as a professional player in 1965 just as Jock Stein was taking over the managerial helm.

Stein soon decided that Craig was his preferred right back over the likes of Willie O'Neill and Iain Young. O'Neill and Young were full backs of the old school who rarely ventured above the halfway line, but Stein saw he could mould Craig into a modern attacking full back. The young dental student was now destined to sink his teeth into a greater path to glory.

Jim's parents - James Forbes McIntyre Craig and Margaret Hughes

James Forbes McIntyre Craig was born on 27 August 1910 at 209 Great Junction Street, Leith, Edinburgh to father also named James Forbes McIntyre Craig, an engineer, and mother Lillias Foreman. The birth was registered by James's father James on 15 September 1910 at the Leith Registry Office. It is likely that James was raised in the Evangelical

Session Church in Leith. After leaving school in Leith, James became a drapery salesman.

However, at the outbreak of WWII, James enlisted as a seaman in the Royal Navy. By early 1942 Britain had become isolated from Hitler's European Third Reich and the United States had only recently entered the war after the Japanese attack on Pearl Harbor, Hawaii on 7 December 1941. Britain's Home Fleet was effectively holed up in Scapa Flow, Orkney. It also had a huge presence with the Clyde Fleet, anchored on the River Clyde. Naval vessels had to come into the Clyde shipyards for routine maintenance and refitting, including into the famous Govan shipyards. This effectively threw the young Leith-born Able Seaman James Craig into a chance meeting with a local Govan girl Margaret Hughes.

On 28 June 1914 the Archduke Franz Ferdinand of the Austro-Hungarian Empire was assassinated in Sarajevo by Serbian dissident Gavrilo Princip. This seemingly inauspicious act of terrorism was the catalyst for the outbreak of WWI in August 1914. During the next four years of conflict, it led to the slaughter of tens of millions of humans around the world. On that very same day in infamy a piece of the jigsaw in the history of the Lisbon Lions was put into place.

Margaret Hughes was born on 28 June 1914 at 12 Harmony Row, Govan, Glasgow to father Patrick Hughes, a ship caulker in the world-renowned Govan shipyards, and mother Annie Bridget Wisdom. The birth was registered by Margaret's father Patrick on 6 July 1914 at the Glasgow Registry Office.

Harmony Row in Govan was also very much associated with arguably the greatest football manager to be produced among a pantheon of Scottish greats; and his name was not Jock Stein, Matt Busby or Bill Shankly. As a boy he played for his local team Harmony Row FC in Govan and went on to sign for the Glasgow Rangers, but his greatest achievements in football were as manager of Aberdeen in the 1980s and the mighty Manchester United team between 1986 and 2013. His name is Sir Alex Ferguson and he remains the patron of Harmony Row FC.

Margaret was raised in the Roman Catholic faith and attended St Anthony's RC Church in Langlands Road in Govan. Margaret would have known little about the Great War but World War II was to play a significant role in her life. Margaret was in her late 20s by that time and it may have crossed her mind that she could be 'left on the shelf'. However, history decreed that this was not to be the case for Margaret. At that time she was working as a cashier for the Welfare Department and living with her parents at 222 Drumoyne Road, Govan when she met a young seaman based with the huge Royal Naval fleet anchored in the Clyde basin.

In those dark days of wartime lives were being quickly lost or men and women in love were suddenly wrenched apart at a moment's notice. Courtships tended to be like in the movies - 'A Brief Encounter' - and James and Margaret quickly decided to wed. James Forbes McIntyre Craig, 31, a drapery salesman, engaged in war service as a Seaman Royal Navy, his home address still 209 Great Junction Street, Leith, Edinburgh married wife Margaret Hughes, 27, a Welfare Department cashier, residing at 222 Drumoyne Road, Govan on 28 March 1942 at St Anthony's Chapel, Glasgow according to the forms of the Roman Catholic Church. The wedding was conducted by Father Bartholomew Burns, RC clergyman at St Anthony's; the witnesses were Philip and Anna Hughes, Margaret's brother and sister.

As the war raged on across the globe, Margaret soon fell pregnant with their son Jim. Their son James Philip Craig was born on 30 April 1943 at his grandparents' home at 222 Drumoyne Road, Govan. The birth was registered by Jim's father James on 1 May 1943 at the Glasgow Registry Office.

Jim's paternal grandparents – James Forbes McIntyre Craig and Lillias Foreman

Jim's paternal grandfather James Forbes McIntyre Craig was born around 1874 in South Leith, Edinburghshire to father John Nelson Craig, a blacksmith journeyman, and mother Harriet Lindsay. In 1881 census James, age 7, a scholar, resided at 24 Kirkgate, South Leith with his parents and siblings. Jim's paternal grandmother Lillias Foreman was also born around 1874 in the neighbouring suburb of North Leith to father Thomas Foreman, a seaman in the Merchant Service, and mother Jane Wright. In 1881 census Lillias, also age 7, a scholar, resided at 47 Commercial Street with her parents and her siblings.

James Forbes McIntyre Craig, 22, an iron turner, residing at 30 Lorne Street, Leith married wife Lillias Foreman, also 22, a printer compositor, residing at 18 Bowling Green Street, Leith on Hogmanay, 31 December 1897 at 122 Bonnington Road, Leith according to the forms of the Evangelical Session Church. The wedding was conducted by Rev Charles

Richardson; the best man was Alexander Reid and the best maid was Annie Innes.

Their son, also named James Forbes McIntyre Craig, was born on 27 August 1910 at 209 Great Junction Street, Leith. The birth was registered by James's father James on 15 September 1910 at the Leith Registry Office. Both James Forbes McIntyre Craig, an engine fitter journeyman, and his wife Lillias were still alive in 1942, during WWII, when their son James, serving in the Royal Navy, married Margaret Hughes in Govan, Glasgow.

Jim's maternal grandparents – Patrick Hughes and Annie Bridget Wisdom

Jim's maternal grandfather Patrick Hughes was born around 1885 in Govan, Glasgow to father Philip Hughes, a shipyard worker, and mother Elizabeth Welsh. Jim's maternal grandmother Annie Bridget Wisdom, aka Anna, was born around 1887 in Ireland to father Thomas Wisdom, an iron driller, and mother Margaret Flynn. Ironically, Jim Craig's great-grandfather Thomas was an iron driller named Wisdom and Jim went on to use his own wisdom to graduate from Glasgow University as a wisdom tooth driller!

After leaving school Patrick went into the famous Govan shipyards to work as a ship caulker; a caulker was employed in sealing gaps in the ship's planking and boiler fittings with tarry fibrous materials to make the ship watertight. When Patrick went into the shipyards in the late Victorian era most boats and ships were still wooden in their main construction or decking.

Patrick Hughes, 24, a ship caulker journeyman, residing at 22 Queen Street, Govan, Glasgow married wife Annie Bridget Wisdom, 22, a pawnbroker's assistant, residing at 874 Govan Road, Govan on 27 September 1909 at St Anthony's Chapel, Govan according to the forms of the Roman Catholic Church. The wedding was conducted by Father G McBrearty, RC clergyman; the best man was John Hughes, Patrick's brother, and the best maid was Mary Ellen Wisdom, Annie's sister. Father G McBrearty of St Anthony's also features in Joe McBride's family history in Chapter 13, thus giving him a unique place in the history of the Lisbon Lions.

Patrick and Annie had three known children; son Philip (b. ~1910), daughters Margaret (b. 1914) and Anna. Their daughter Margaret Hughes born on 28 June 1914 at 12 Harmony Row, Govan. The birth was registered by Margaret's father Patrick Hughes on 6 July 1914 at the Glasgow Registry Office. In 1911 census Patrick Hughes, 26, a boiler caulker, resided at 12 Harmony Row, Govan with wife Annie, 24, and baby son Philip, 11 months old. Both Patrick and Anna were still alive in 1942, during WWII, when their daughter Margaret married husband James Craig in Govan.

Jim's great-grandparents

On Jim's paternal line his great-grandfather John Nelson Craig, a blacksmith journeyman, was born around 1838 in Leith, Edinburghshire and his great-grandmother Harriet Lindsay was born around 1841 in Kinghorn in the Kingdom of Fife. John and Harriet had four known children including their son James Forbes McIntyre Craig (b. ~1874). By 1881 John was working as a railway porter in South Leith, almost certainly for the North British Railway Company. In 1881 census John N Craig, 43, a railway porter, resided at 24 Kirkgate, South Leith with wife Harriet, 40, children John, 15, an apprentice wood moulder, then Mary, 12, and James, 7, both at school, and baby William, 3. John Nelson Craig, a blacksmith to trade, and wife Harriet were both still alive in 1897 and living in Leith.

Jim's other paternal great-grandfather Thomas Foreman, a seaman in the Merchant Service, was born around 1833 in the small port of West Wemyss, Fife and his great-grandmother Jane Wright was born around 1843 in Galatown, Dysart, Fife and they had four known children including their daughter Lillias Foreman (b. ~1874). In 1881 census Thomas. 48, a seaman, resided at 47 Commercial Street, North Leith with wife Jane, 38, children Ann, 15, a compositor, Thomas, 13, then Jane, 11, and Lillias, 7, both scholars, William, 5, Margaret, also 5, possibly twins, and baby David, 2. By the end of the 19th century Thomas, still working as a merchant seaman, and his wife Jane were still living and working in Leith. At that time, the Port of Leith was a busy, bustling harbour with ships serving all parts of Western Europe, Scandinavia and the Baltic ports.

On Jim's maternal line was his great-grandfather Philip Hughes, a shipyard labourer, and his great-grandmother was Elizabeth Welsh and they had two known sons; Patrick (b. ~1885) and John. Coincidentally, Chapter 15 will concentrate on another Lion, John 'Yogi' Hughes, descended from a separate Hughes' lineage. Jim's other maternal great-grandfather was Thomas Wisdom, an iron driller, and his great-grand-mother was Margaret Flynn and they had two known daughters Annie Bridget (b. ~1887) and Mary Ellen. It is likely that the Hughes and Wisdom families, who in the early 20th century were living and working in the shadow of the fast expanding Govan shipyards, were in the main, descendants of Irish immigrants.

Chapter 3

Tommy Gemmell (left back)

Honours as a Celtic player:

1 European Cup

6 Scottish League titles

3 Scottish Cups

4 Scottish League Cups

The young Tommy Gemmell

Tommy Gemmell became a Celtic legend on that famous night of 25 May 1967. It seemed the first goal scored by the defensively-minded Inter Milan would have been enough to win them the European Cup. However, Jock Stein's tactics had developed Jim Craig and Tommy Gemmell into modern attacking full backs bypassing the midfield and linking up with the forward line. On one of those foraging runs down the left Gemmell, screaming for a cutback from Jim Craig on the right, struck a thunderbolt shot into the back of the dumbstruck Italians' net. Tommy was immortalised by scoring that equalising goal, which brought Celtic back into the final and ultimately into the ascendancy in the game.

Thomas Gemmell was born on 16 October 1943, again during WWII, at 72 Cumbrae Drive, Dalziel, Motherwell to father Alfred Gemmell, an engineer turner, and mother

Margaret Miller Stewart. The birth was registered by Tommy's father Alfred on 19 October 1943 at the Motherwell Registry Office. Tommy was born in his granny's home in Cumbrae Drive, Motherwell and he was raised in the Protestant faith.

When Tommy was five years old the Gemmell family moved to nearby Craigneuk in Wishaw. In his youth, Tommy was a big Motherwell FC fan, growing up in the tough industrial environment that was South Lanarkshire with its grim, unforgiving coal mines and foreboding iron and steel works. Tommy had a reputation as a hard and uncompromising full back on the playing field, something he would have learned growing up in the harsh Lanarkshire conditions which his forebears had to endure.

As a boy Tommy played as a right back for his school team and only moved to left back when his amateur team Meadow Thistle were short of a full back. He joined Celtic from junior club Coltness United in 1961, although he had already been training with the Parkhead club two evenings per week. Tommy was signed by Jimmy McGrory for Celtic on the same evening as Jimmy Johnstone and the pair became great friends.

Tommy's parents – Alfred Gemmell and Margaret Miller Stewart

In 1922 Alfred Gemmell was born about an hour before his twin sister Winifred and they were registered as Nos. 100 and 101 respectively in the register of births for Bellshill. Alfred was born on 24 January 1922 at 348 Main Street, Bellshill, Lanarkshire to father Thomas Gemmell, a boiler fireman, and mother Elizabeth Stewart Hamilton. The births for Alfred and Winifred were registered by their father Thomas on 6 February 1922 at the Bellshill Registry Office. After leaving school Alfred trained as an apprentice engineer turner, working in one of the proliferation of engineering works in Scotland's industrial heartland of Lanarkshire at that time and he continued to work there in a 'protected occupation' at the outbreak of WWII.

Tommy's mother Margaret Miller Stewart was born on 21 June 1923 at 5 Glenpark Terrace, Eastfield, in the Royal burgh of Rutherglen, to father David Stewart, a steel worker, and mother Mary Gorman. The birth was registered by Margaret's father David on 6 July 1923 at the Rutherglen Registry Office. By September 1939 when Margaret was still only 16, the Nazis had marched into Poland and Britain quickly entered the growing conflict. Margaret was soon employed in war service along with many young women in the multitude of munitions factories spread across Glasgow and Lanarkshire. The author's own grandmother Annie Collie also worked in a munitions factory in Thornliebank during the same period as Margaret. This was hard and dangerous work for young girls, with the threat of explosives going off and the factories were also prime targets for Luftwaffe bombing raids. In 1943 while working in the munitions factory Margaret met young engineer turner Alfred Gemmell and she fell pregnant with Tommy.

Alfred Gemmell, 21, an engineer turner, residing at 348 Main Street, Bellshill married wife Margaret Miller Stewart,

20, a munitions worker, residing at 72 Cumbrae Drive, Dalziel, Motherwell on 27 August 1943 at Holy Trinity Church, Motherwell according to the forms of the Episcopal Church. The wedding was conducted by Father M Coyle, clergyman of Holy Trinity; the witnesses were Francis and Anna Todd of 684 Merry Street, Motherwell. Their son Thomas was born on 16 October 1943 at 72 Cumbrae Drive, Dalziel, Motherwell. The birth was registered by Tommy's father Alfred on 19 October 1943 at the Motherwell Registry Office. In 1948 the Gemmell family moved to live in Craigneuk in Wishaw.

Tommy's paternal grandparents – Thomas Gemmell and Elizabeth Stewart Hamilton

Tommy's paternal grandfather Thomas Gemmell was born around 1877 in Paisley, Renfrewshire to father Henry Gemmell, a navigational man, and mother Agnes Houston. In 1881 census Thomas, 4, resided at 5 Thread Street, Paisley with his parents and his widowed great-grandfather who was also named Thomas Gemmell. Tommy's paternal grandmother Elizabeth Stewart Hamilton was born around 1881 in Kilbirnie, Ayrshire to father David Hamilton, a scotcher in a thread-mill, and mother Janet Smellie. In 1881 census Elizabeth, 10, a scholar, resided at Main Street, Kilbirnie with her parents and siblings including her twin sister Catherine, also 10. Twin children appear to be a genetic feature of the Gemmell family line.

Thomas and Elizabeth both met and fell in love in the small town of Kilbirnie in Ayrshire. Thomas Gemmell, 21, a general labourer, residing at Bridgend, Kilbirnie married wife Elizabeth Stewart Hamilton, 17, a mill worker, on April Fools' Day, 1 April 1898 at Elizabeth's home according to the forms of the Church of Scotland. The wedding was conducted by Rev Thomas Buchan; the best man was Charles Closs and the best maid was Catherine Benbeth Hamilton, Elizabeth's twin sister.

By the 1920s Thomas, working as a boiler fireman, had moved with Elizabeth to live in Bellshill, Lanarkshire, and in 1922 they had twins Alfred and Winifred. Thomas and Elizabeth's son Alfred Gemmell was born at 5pm and daughter Winifred was born an hour later at 6pm on 24 January 1922 at 348 Main Street, Bellshill, Lanarkshire. The births were registered by the twins' father Thomas on 6 February 1922 at the Bellshill Registry Office. In 1943, during WWII, Thomas Gemmell, an engineer's labourer, was recorded as a widower and his wife Elizabeth was dead by then.

Tommy's maternal grandparents – David Stewart and Mary Gorman

Tommy's maternal grandfather David Stewart was born around 1884 in the burgh of Glasgow to father John Stewart, a paper maker operative, and mother Annie Robertson. In 1891 census David, 6, a scholar, resided at 15 Union Place, Wardlawhill, Rutherglen with his parents and siblings. Tommy's maternal grandmother Mary Gorman was born around 1890 in Cambuslang to Irish-born parents Joseph Gorman, a gardener, and mother Anna Johnstone. In 1891 census Mary, only 1 year old, resided in a small tenement at Russell's Land, Rutherglen with her parents, five siblings and two boarders. In those days the parents would sleep in a bed recess and the children all tended to sleep in the same bed. Boarders would have to make do and mend, a bed usually being shared in shifts.

Seven months after Armistice Day in WWI, David, who had been married previously and was by then a widower, and his second wife Mary married in the Royal burgh of Rutherglen. David Stewart, 35, a widowed steel worker, residing at 32 Dukes Road, Cambuslang married Mary Gorman, 29, an insurance agent, residing at 4 Glenpark Terrace, Eastfield, Rutherglen at Mary's home on 11 July 1919 according to the forms of the Church of Scotland. Their daughter Margaret Miller Stewart was born on 21 June 1923 at 5 Glenpark Terrace, Eastfield, Rutherglen. The birth was registered by Margaret's father David on 6 July 1923 at the Rutherglen Registry Office. David Stewart, a cable layer, and his wife Mary were still alive in 1943, during WWII, when their daughter Margaret married Alfred Gemmell.

Tommy's great-grandparents

Tommy's great-grandparents were all born around the middle part of the 19th century. On Tommy's paternal line his great-grandfather Henry Gemmell, a navigation man, was born around 1856. His great-grandmother Agnes Houston was born around 1857 both in the weaving town of Paisley, Renfrewshire, famed for its Paisley pattern shawls and thread works, and their son was Thomas Gemmell (b. ~1877, Paisley). A navigation man sounds quite a grand occupation for Henry Gemmell, however, it was a common term used for a manual labourer employed to work on the roads, railways and canals. It was commonly abbreviated to the form 'navvy' and over time an 'Irish navvy' became a term of derision.

However, prior to Henry becoming a navvy it appears that he tried his hand as a confectioner. In 1881 census Henry Gemmell, 25, a confectioner, resided at 5 Thread Street, Paisley with wife Agnes, 24, son Thomas, 4, and Henry's widowed grandfather Thomas Gemmell, 73, a weaver. This meant Tommy Gemmell's great-great-great-grandfather was also Thomas Gemmell and he was born in Paisley around 1808. In Watson's Directory of 1882-83 for Paisley and Renfrewshire Henry Gemmell was listed in the Paisley section as follows: *'Gemmell, Henry, confectioner, 16 Wallace street'*.

Tommy's other paternal great-grandfather David Hamilton, a scotcher in a thread-mill, was born around 1853 in the small mill town of Kilbirnie, Ayrshire and his great-grandmother was Janet Smellie. David and Janet had 7 known children including twin daughters Catherine and Elizabeth Stewart Hamilton (b. ~1881). By 1891 David's young wife Janet was dead, probably in childbirth the previous year, after having given birth to a son Robert in 1890.

In 1891 census widower David Hamilton, 38, a linen thread dresser, resided at Main Street, Kilbirnie with children John, 15, a steelwork labourer, Alexander, 13, a linen thread reeler, twin scholars Catherine, 10, and Elizabeth, 10, David, 7, also at school, Janet, 4, and baby son Robert, only 11 months old. By the end of the 19th century the Gemmell and Hamilton families were still living and working in Kilbirnie.

On Tommy's maternal line his great-grandfather John Stewart, a paper maker operative, was born around 1846 in Glasgow and his great-grandmother Annie Stewart Robertson, aka Ann, was born around 1850 in Stirling, Stirlingshire. John and Annie had 6 known children including son David (b. ~1884, Glasgow). By the beginning of the 1890s the Stewart family had moved from the burgh of Glasgow to Rutherglen and John almost certainly worked at the huge Clyde Paper Works Ltd which was opened in 1852 in Eastfield, Rutherglen and which operated right up until 1971 as the Clyde Paper Mills.

In 1891 census John Stewart, 45, a paper maker, resided at 15 Union Place, Wardlawhill, Rutherglen with wife Ann, 41, children Archibald, 13, Ann, 10, George, 8, David, 6, all scholars, William, 3, and baby Elizabeth, only 6 months old. A 29 year-old tube cutter, probably related to John, named Robert Stewart, recorded as being born in the East Indies, was also boarding there. In 1919 John, a retired paper-maker, and Annie were still alive and living in Cambuslang, Lanarkshire.

Tommy's other maternal great-grandfather Joseph Gorman, a gardener, was born in Ireland around 1853, just after the devastating Irish Potato Famine (1848-52). His great-grandmother Anna Johnstone, aka Annie, was born about two years later in 1855 also in Ireland. Joseph and Annie had 6 known children including daughter Mary (b. ~1890, Cambuslang). In 1891 Joseph Gorman, 38, a gardener, resided at Russell's Land, Rutherglen with wife Annie, 36, a gardener's wife, children William, 15, a grocer's boy, Joseph, 13, a flesher's boy (an old term for a butcher's boy), then Lizzie Jane, 11,

Maggie, 7, James, 5, all scholars, and baby Mary, 1. Joseph had also taken in a couple of unmarried boarders into his small, cramped two-windowed tenement home; Charles Richards, 35, a brewer's labourer, stated as born in Italy and Irish-born John Queen, 33, a coal miner. In 1919, Joseph and Anna were still alive and living in Eastfield, Rutherglen, which lies close to Cambuslang.

Chapter 4

Bobby Murdoch (right half)

Honours as a Celtic player:

1 European Cup

8 Scottish League titles

5 Scottish Cups

5 Scottish League Cups

The young Bobby Murdoch

Bobby Murdoch was born 10 weeks after the D-Day landings, which took place on the beaches of Normandy in France and was the defining turning point in WWII, signalling the final Allied advance against Adolf Hitler's Third Reich. Robert White Murdoch was born on 17 August 1944 at 57 Toryglen Road, Rutherglen, Glasgow to father Robert White Murdoch, a steelworks furnaceman, and mother Barbara MacDonald. The birth was registered by Bobby's father Robert on 31 August 1944 at the Rutherglen Registry Office.

Bobby was raised in the Royal burgh of Rutherglen and he lived there for most of his life. He attended St. Columbkille's Primary School there, before moving on to Our Lady's High Secondary in Motherwell. It was while studying there and aged only 14 that Bobby played in the same school football

First XI as Billy McNeill. When Bobby left Our Lady's he became a sheet-metal worker, following his father Robert into the tough environment of the Lanarkshire steelworks.

Bobby signed for Celtic in August 1959 as a £3-a-week part-timer while still working at the sheet-metal works. He continued to gain experience playing for his local junior side Cambuslang Rangers, before joining the Parkhead club permanently in 1961. Aged 19 and living at 30 Lochlea Road, Rutherglen, Bobby married wife Kathleen on 6 June 1964 at St Mark's RC Church. As one of the Lions, Bobby Murdoch will always be remembered for firing in the vital shot on goal which Stevie Chalmers, well placed in the Italians' penalty box, guided in to win the Hoops the European Cup.

A story the author recalled from his railway accounting days in 1985 was told to him by his old boss, the now sadly deceased John Clark, who was Area Freight Manager at Motherwell Depot. Not to be confused with the Lisbon Lion to be discussed later, John Clark, who was also a massive Celtic fan, related that in his youth, he was also a pretty decent footballer. John eagerly stated that as a young lad he went down to Middlesbrough FC to train with the English team on a trial basis.

Bobby Murdoch had transferred to Middlesbrough in 1973 and John was in awe training alongside his Celtic hero, who had become Middlesbrough's youth coach. A young Graeme Souness also came under Murdoch's guiding wing at that time. However, John, who would later gain a reputation as a hard, uncompromising manager in the railway, became an unhappy, homesick youngster and he returned to Motherwell, effectively ending his aspirations to become a professional footballer. John Clark may not be in heaven but he certainly is in Paradise!

Bobby's parents – Robert White Murdoch and Barbara MacDonald

Robert White Murdoch was born on 29 July 1919 at 45 Richard Street, Anderston, Glasgow to father Matthew Watson Murdoch, a ship yard labourer, and mother Sarah White. The birth was registered by Robert's father Matthew on 15 August 1919 at the Glasgow Registry Office. Robert was raised in the Roman Catholic faith and after leaving school he got a job as a steelwork furnaceman. By the time WWII broke out the Murdoch family resided in Bridgeton, Glasgow.

Barbara MacDonald was born on 16 October 1923 at 22 Greenhill Road, Rutherglen, Glasgow to father William MacDonald, a carter, and mother Mary Kelly. The birth was registered by Barbara's father William on 22 October 1923 at the Rutherglen Registry Office. Barbara was raised in the Protestant faith. During WWII, Barbara worked in a munitions factory when she met her future sweetheart Robert.

Robert Murdoch, 24, a steelwork furnaceman, residing at 37 Lily Street, Bridgeton, Glasgow married wife Barbara MacDonald, 21, a munitions worker, residing at 57 Toryglen Road, Rutherglen on Hogmanay, 31 December 1943, at Sacred Heart Church, Bridgeton according to the forms of the Roman Catholic Church. The wedding was conducted by Father Anthony Mullins, priest at Sacred Heart; the witnesses were John and Mary Murdoch, Robert's brother and sister, both also of 37 Lily Street.

Robert and Barbara's son Robert White Murdoch was born on 17 August 1944 at 57 Toryglen Road, Rutherglen. The birth was registered by Bobby's father Robert on 31 August 1944 at the Rutherglen Registry Office. Robert White Murdoch, a boiler cleaner, and wife Barbara were still alive in 1964 when Bobby married his wife Kathleen in St Mark's Church.

Bobby's paternal grandparents – Matthew Watson Murdoch and Sarah White

Bobby's paternal grandfather Matthew Watson Murdoch was born around 1895 in Glasgow to father John McDonald Murdoch, a marine fireman, and mother Elizabeth Fisher McLean. In 1901 census Matthew, 6, a scholar, resided at 56 McAlpine Street, Broomielaw, Glasgow with his parents and his four brothers. Bobby's paternal grandmother Sarah White was born around 1894 in Glasgow to Irish-born parents Robert White, an iron dresser, and Mary McGory. In 1901 census Sarah, 7, a scholar, resided at Back Land, 56 Carrick Street, Broomielaw, Glasgow with her parents and siblings. The postal description of 'Back Land' is very much an old Scottish term where land means a tenement building and the back was the term used to describe the drying green area at the rear, so the postman would know that the White family resided at the rear of the tenement.

In 1914 Matthew and Sarah were both living in Anderston, Glasgow when they married. Matthew Watson Murdoch, 18, a coal trimmer, residing at 453 Argyle Street, Anderston,

Glasgow married wife Sarah White, 19, a bolt screwer, residing at 45 Richard Street, Anderston on New Year's Day, 1 January 1914 at St Patrick's Church, Anderston according to the forms of the Roman Catholic Church. The wedding was conducted by Father Andrew Lynch; the best man was David Lavery and the best maid was Mary Shades.

Matthew and Sarah had 3 known children; Robert, John and Mary. Their son Robert White Murdoch was born on 29 July 1919 at 45 Richard Street, Anderston. The birth was registered by Robert's father Matthew on 15 August 1919 at the Glasgow Registry Office. Matthew, a dock labourer, and Sarah were still alive in 1944, during WWII, and living at 37 Lily Street, Bridgeton when their son Robert married wife Barbara.

Bobby's maternal grandparents – William MacDonald and Mary Kelly

Bobby's maternal grandfather William MacDonald was born around 1892 to father James MacDonald, a county council lamplighter, and mother Barbara Hart. Bobby's maternal grandmother Mary Kelly was born around 1895 to father John Kelly, a wire rope-maker operative, and mother Mary Ann Moran. After leaving school William became a corporation lamplighter like his father before him. This was in the days before electric street lighting and tenement close and gas street lights had to be lit manually. After her schooling Mary worked in a local pottery works.

Four months before the outbreak of WWI, William and Mary married in the Royal burgh of Rutherglen. William

MacDonald, 22, a corporation lamplighter, residing at 6 Greenhill Road, Rutherglen married Mary Kelly, 19, a pottery worker, residing at 278 King Street, Rutherglen on 17 April 1914 at the Manse, Rutherglen according to the forms of the Church of Scotland. The wedding was conducted by Rev William Vallance, minister of Rutherglen West Parish Church; the best man was James Kerr and the best maid was Mary Sweeney.

By 1923 William was no longer a lamplighter and he was working as a carter. William and Mary's daughter Barbara MacDonald was born on 16 October 1923 at 22 Greenhill Road, Rutherglen. The birth was registered by Barbara's father William on 22 October 1923 at the Rutherglen Registry Office. William, a labourer, and Mary were still alive in 1944 and living at 57 Toryglen Road, Rutherglen when their daughter Barbara married husband Robert Murdoch.

Bobby's great-grandparents

Bobby's great-grandparents were all born around the 1850s and 60s. On Bobby's paternal line his bilingual great-grandfather John McDonald Murdoch, a marine fireman, was born around 1851 in Inverness, and he spoke Gaelic and English. A marine fireman stoked coal down in the hot, dark, sweaty engine rooms of coal fired steamships. Bobby's great-grandmother Elizabeth Fisher McLean was born around 1857 in Glasgow. John and Elizabeth had five known sons including Matthew Watson Murdoch (b. ~1895).

In 1901 John Murdoch, 50, a ship's stoker, resided at 56 McAlpine Street, Broomielaw, Glasgow with wife Elizabeth, 44, sons William, 23, a baker's apprentice, Donald, 18, a painter's apprentice, George, 16, a van boy, Edward, 10, and Matthew, 6, both scholars. As a ship's stoker at the end of the Victorian era, John Murdoch would never be short of work. The Broomielaw Docks on the River Clyde was always bustling with cargo vessels and a multitude of passenger steamers, which provided the hard-pressed Glasgow folk with their most popular pastime – taking a trip 'Doon the Watter'. By the beginning of 1914 John was dead and his wife Elizabeth was a widow.

Bobby's other paternal great-grandfather Robert White, an iron dresser, was born around 1863 and his great-grandmother Mary McGory was born about 1864 both in Ireland. Robert and Mary emigrated to Glasgow in the 1880s and they had four children there, including daughter Sarah (b. ~1894). In 1901 census Robert White, 38, an iron dresser, resided at Back Land, 56 Carrick Street, Broomielaw, Glasgow with wife Mary, 37, an unemployed pottery worker, children Robert, 17, a foundry labourer, Sarah, 7, a scholar, Mary Jane, 4, and Rose Ann, 2. By the beginning of 1914 Robert White was dead and his widow Mary had remarried her second husband, surnamed Evans.

On Bobby's maternal line was his great-grandfather James MacDonald, a county council lamplighter, and his great-grandmother was Barbara Hart and they had a son William (b. ~1892). In 1914 James, a lamplighter, and Barbara were still alive and living at 6 Greenhill Road, Rutherglen. Bobby's other maternal great-grandfather was John Kelly, a wire rope maker operative, and his great-grandmother was Mary Ann Moran and they had a daughter Mary (b. ~1895).

In 1914 John Kelly was a widower as his wife Mary Ann had died and John was living at 278 King Street, Rutherglen.

Chapter 5

Billy McNeill (Captain and centre half)

Honours as a Celtic player:

1 European Cup
9 Scottish League titles
7 Scottish Cups
6 Scottish League Cups

The young Billy McNeill

William McNeill, aka Billy, was born on 2 March 1940, against the backdrop of the early dark days of WWII, at 116 Main Street, Bellshill, Lanarkshire, which was his maternal grandparents' miner's cottage. His father was Sergeant (Physical Training Instructor) James McNeill attached to the Army Physical Training Corps and his mother was Ellen Mitchell. Although Billy's father was a serving soldier engaged in war service, Jimmy was able to be present at his son's birth, and he registered the birth on 15 March 1940 at the Bellshill Registry Office.

Billy's Lithuanian grandparents had boarded an immigrant ship believing that they were destined for New York and instead they landed in the port of Leith near Edinburgh. Billy remembered his grandparents as very proud and kind people. Many years later, in October 1967, on a European Cup second leg trip with Celtic to play Dinamo Kiev, the local journalists were keen to interview Billy about his Lithu-anian heritage, but he confessed to knowing very little about this part of his family history. Of course, Kiev is actually the capital of Ukraine, with Vilnius being the capital of Lithua-nia. However, it must be remembered that Ukraine and Lith-uania were still part of the Union of Soviet Socialist Republics (USSR) at that time and they had been part of Tsarist Russia before 1917, so the TASS state-sponsored journalists would be interviewing Billy from a Moscow-centric viewpoint.

Billy was born in his Lithuanian grandparents' house in Bellshill and the McNeill family lived there along with his Auntie Grace in the miner's row until he was six. Three years later, when Billy was nine, the family moved to Hereford Barracks to be with his father Jimmy. At school in Here-ford, Billy was introduced to rugby football, which he really enjoyed and he was quite handy with the oval ball. However, Billy wrote that he was delighted when the McNeill family returned to Lanarkshire and he attended Our Lady's High School in Motherwell, which had a great footballing tradi-tion. The round ball was what Billy wanted to play with most and he did so with great distinction.

Billy's father Jimmy was not a big football fan, but Billy's uncle Frank from Dundee was a big Dundee United fan. When Billy's father was serving in West Africa his aunt Grace first introduced Billy to Glasgow Celtic at the age of nine. He paid his first visit to Celtic Park on 15 October 1949 when the Hoops beat Aberdeen 4-2. That team boasted Mike Haughney and Charlie Tully, who greatly impressed the young Billy. Also on the field that day were Bobby Evans and Bobby Collins, two players who were briefly Billy's team-mates at Celtic.

When Billy was 17 he played for Our Lady's High School against Holyrood Secondary -which was the author's mother Margaret McCue's old school - at Hampden Park in his first national cup final. Unfortunately, Billy scored an own goal that day and the game ended 1-1, with no replay ever having been rearranged. Over the next couple of years several clubs scouted on Billy, including Arsenal, Manchester United, Newcastle, Clyde and Partick.

However, after playing for Scotland Schoolboys against England at Celtic Park and winning 3-0, Jock Stein, who watched the game, had immediate talks with Sir Robert Kelly, the Celtic chairman. Stein accompanied Eddie McCardle, the Celtic scout, to Billy's home and terms were quickly concluded for the youngster to join Celtic from Blantyre Victoria in May 1957. A legendary captain, who earned the nickname Cesar, was in the making and the road to Lisbon was in his destiny.

Billy's parents - James McNeill and Ellen Mitchell

In the spring of 1914 the dark thunderclouds of war were spreading across Imperialist Europe, although at that time little of this was of major concern to the British populace. In the Tayside city of Dundee the main concerns would have been regarding the production levels of jute, the material which was the main industry in Dundee at that time. In fact, production of jute would soar during WWI. It was used in soldiers' uniforms, belts, webbing, satchels and many other military uses.

Billy's father was born in that early spring of 1914 in Dundee. James McNeill, aka Jimmy, was born illegitimately on 6 March 1914 at 60 Kemback Street, St Andrew's, Dundee to father William McNeill, a lorry driver, and mother Margaret McArthur, a jute spinner. The birth was registered by Jimmy's mother Margaret, who signed with her 'x' mark, and father William, residing at 60 Kemback Street on 23 March 1914 at the Dundee Registry Office. Jimmy's parents were actually cohabiting as common law husband and wife and more will be discussed about the reasons for this later. Jimmy was only four years old when 'the war to end all wars' ended in 1918.

If anyone breaks the mould in terms of the myth of the Bhoys, who reportedly came from a 30 square mile radius of Celtic Park, then it must be Billy's mother Ellen Mitchell. Ellen's roots stretch back to Eastern Europe when Lithuania was part of the Tsarist Russian Empire and the doomed Nicholas and Alexandra were still on the Russian throne. Between 1868, when Lithuania was struck by a great famine, and the start of WWI in 1914, more than 635,000 Lithuanians emigrated to Russia, Western Europe and the USA, representing about 20% of the population. Ellen Mitchell's parents were part of that great migration and they came to the Lanarkshire coalfields seeking employment and economic security, although originally they were heading for the USA.

Ellen was born Alene Walatkeviczus on 29 July 1917 at 11 Muirpark Rows, Bellshill to father Kazis Walatkeviczus, a coal miner, and mother Urzula Jurkeniute. The birth was registered by her father Kazis, who signed with his 'x' mark, on 30 July 1917 at the Bellshill Registry Office. On the following day, 31 July 1917, the British and Allied forces launched the Battle of Ypres with an attack at Pilckem Ridge on Flanders Field in Belgium and the dreadful slaughter of the Great War rolled on.

Lithuania had been under German occupation since 1915, however, in September 1917, Germany allowed a conference in Vilnius to be held to discuss Lithuanian independence, under German alliance. The Council of Lithuania, led by Jonas Basanavicius, declared Lithuanian independence under a German protectorate on 11 December 1917, however, following German losses on the Western Front, outright independence was declared on 16 February 1918.

Ellen, not even one year old, would have been oblivious to the momentous events in her parents' homeland. In fact, the Walatkeviczus family had no intention of returning to the newly independent Lithuania and, like many immigrants, they changed their name to the anglicized surname of Mitchell and Alene grew up as Ellen Mitchell.

By the time Jimmy and Ellen were ready to marry at the end of 1938 the storm clouds of war in Europe were beginning to erupt again and by that time Jimmy was a professional soldier in the famous Black Watch regiment. He rose to be a tough and uncompromising Sergeant in the Army Physical Training Corps. James McNeill, 24, a physical training instructor, residing at 508 Main Street, Mossend, Lanarkshire married wife Ellen Mitchell, 21, residing at 116 Main Street, Bellshill on Hogmanay, 31 December 1938, at the Holy Family Church, Mossend according to the forms of the Roman Catholic Church. The wedding was conducted by Father Les Power and the witnesses were Stanley Bungard and Grace Mitchell, Ellen's sister.

The marriage was registered on 4 January 1939 at the Bellshill Registry Office and nine months later on 3 September 1939, Jimmy was called up for war service and continued in his role as a PTI instructor. Jimmy and Ellen's son Billy was born the following year on 2 March 1940 at Jimmy's in law's miner's cottage at 116 Main Street, Bellshill. Jimmy registered the birth on 15 March 1940 at the Bellshill Registry Office.

This was still towards the end of the period named the 'Phoney War', due to the fact there had been very little direct conflict between Britain and Nazi Germany. This was soon to end and, in fact, the following day on 16 March 1940 German bombers attacked Scapa Flow in Orkney inflicting the first British civilian casualties of WWII. Three months later in June 1940 came the 'Retreat from Dunkirk' and Britain knew it was in the war for real.

After the end of WWII Jimmy continued to serve in the British Army in what was to become a 22-year career as a Sergeant in the Black Watch regiment and the Army Physical Training Corps where he rose to the rank of Warrant Officer. He had postings including West Africa and Hereford in England in the late 1940s and 50s, but after retiring from the army he returned to live in Lanarkshire. Jimmy was not a big football fan, unlike his brother Frank McNeill in Dundee, but he was eminently proud of his son Billy and his achievements with Celtic. Jimmy, a retired soldier in his 84th year, died in 1998, having seen his son Billy achieve so many great honours as a player and manager with Celtic.

Billy's paternal grandparents – William McNeill and Margaret McArthur

Billy McNeill would not have known his paternal grandparents as they both died a decade before he was born. Billy's grandfather William McNeill was born about 1876, possibly in Paisley, Renfrewshire to father James McNeill, a coal miner. Billy's paternal grandmother Margaret McArthur was born illegitimately on 18 June 1876 at 14 Dens Road, Dundee, to mother Jane McArthur, a jute spinner. The birth was registered by Margaret's mother Jane, who signed with her 'x' mark, on 19 July 1876 at the Dundee Registry Office. No father of repute was registered.

Margaret McArthur married a soldier named Private James Bonnett, but it appears that this was an unhappy marriage and by around 1903 Margaret had left Bonnett, who served with the Royal Scots regiment. It is uncertain whether Margaret had met William McNeill at this time, although it is very likely as by 1905 she was pregnant. Son Henry McArthur or Bonnett, aka Harry, was born illegitimately on 11 October 1905 at 17 Baker Lane, St Andrews, Fife to mother Margaret McArthur, a mill worker. Margaret was the wife of 'James Bonnett, Private Royal Scots who she declares is not the father of the child, and further that she had no personal communications with him for 18 months'.

By around late 1906, William McNeill was certainly cohabiting with his common law wife Margaret. William and Margaret were known to have had three sons; Henry, aka Harry, Francis, aka Frank, James, aka Jimmy, and a daughter Williamina. William, a lorryman, and Margaret, a jute spinner like her mother before her, bore their daughter Williamina

McNeill on 22 September 1907 at 25 Hawkhill, Dundee. The birth was registered by mother Margaret Bonnett and father William McNeill on 8 October 1907 at the Dundee Registry Office. Williamina's mother Margaret McArthur was at that time still the wife of Private James Bonnett, a soldier in the Royal Scots regiment, but Margaret again declared Bonnett 'was not the father of her child, and further that she had no communication with him since they ceased to reside together about four years ago'.

The following year William and Margaret's son Frank was born. Francis Lindsay McNeill was born illegitimately on 20 April 1909 at 75 Foundry Lane, Dundee. The birth was registered by mother Margaret and father William, of 3 Crescent Lane, Dundee on 3 May 1909 at the Dundee Registry Office. Billy's uncle Frank in Dundee fervently supported Dundee United, but he followed Celtic when he came to Glasgow to watch Billy play. Frank's younger brother was Billy's father James.

Son James McNeill was born illegitimately on 6 March 1914 at 60 Kemback Street, St Andrew's, Dundee. The birth was registered by Jimmy's mother Margaret, who signed with her 'x' mark, and father William, residing at 60 Kemback Street on 23 March 1914 at the Dundee Registry Office. No mention was made of James Bonnett.

William and Margaret remained in a long term relationship, but the likelihood is that, being Catholic, Margaret could not or would not get a divorce from her soldier husband James Bonnett (one of the 'Bonnet's o' Bonnie Dundee'). Divorce in Catholic families at that time was almost unheard of and would have been a greater scandal for Margaret than cohabiting with William McNeill.

In 1911 census William McNeill, 34, a lorry driver, resided at 7 Crescent Street, Dundee with wife Margaret, 31, a jute spinner, sons Harry, 5, a scholar, Frank, 1, and daughter Williamina, 3. William stated that he had been married for six years, about 1905, but there is no registered evidence of any formal wedding having taken place.

By 1930 both William and Margaret were seriously ill.

Margaret Bonnett or McArthur, only 53, and still recorded as married to James Bonnett, a soldier, died on 20 January 1930 in Dundee Royal Infirmary and the death was registered by her married daughter Williamina Glenday, of 2 Ogilvies Road, on 21 January 1930 at the Dundee Registry Office. It appears that Margaret's estranged husband James Bonnett was still alive in 1930, but William McNeill is not mentioned on the death certificate, which supports the theory that there was never any marriage.

However, Margaret had been living with William at their usual address, which was recorded by daughter Wilhelmina as 90 Albert Street, Dundee. Tragically, William was to die at the same address within six short months of Margaret's passing. William McNeill, only 54, a harbour labourer, recorded as single, died on 6 June 1930 at 90 Albert Street, Dundee and the death was registered once again by his daughter Williamina Glenday on 7 June 1930 at the Dundee Registry Office. A complex affair of the heart had come to an end.

Billy's maternal grandparents – Kazis Walatkeviczus and Urzula Jurkeniute

Billy McNeill knew very little about the origins of his Lithuanian grandparents Kazis Walatkeviczus and Urzula Jurkeniute. As stated previously, Billy confessed to reporters at Kiev
airport after arriving for a Dinamo Kiev v Celtic European
Cup match that he had no idea of where about in Lithuania
Kazis and Urzula originated from, although what is known
is that they came from one of the rural agricultural regions
as opposed to one of the industrial towns. Their parents were
farming folk.

Kazis Walatkeviczus was born about 1884 in Lithuania to
father Mikelaitu Walatkeviczus, a farmer, and mother Marie
Latikavicz. His future wife Urzula Jurkeniute was born
about 1886 in Lithuania to father Anton Jurkeniute, also a
farmer, and mother Agata Jerbulei. In the early 1900s there
was a flood of rural Lithuanian immigrants who arrived in
Scotland, the men mainly looking for work in the extensive
Lanarkshire coalfields. Kazis and Urzula arrived during this
period and it is possible they emigrated together from the
same farming region in Lithuania.

Kazis Walatkeviczus, 25, a coal miner, who signed with his
'x' mark, married wife Urzula Jurkeniute, 23, who also signed
with her 'x' mark, both residing at 55 Bothwellpark Rows,
Bellshill, on 4 January 1909 at the RC Church, Uddingston,
according to the forms of the Roman Catholic Church. The
wedding was conducted by Father William Orr, RC clergyman; the witnesses were Jurgis Tenkauckas and Robert
Traynor.

At the outbreak of the WWI, Lithuania was effectively

allied to Germany and was under German occupation from 1915. The Walatkeviczus family, along with many other Lithuanian families, decided to move towards anglicising their names, much as the Royal Family did in WWI, when they changed the Germanic Saxe-Coburg to Windsor. Eventually, the Walatkeviczus were to change their surnames to Mitchell. In 1901 census a Thomas Mitchell was the tenant at 55 Bothwellpark Rows and it seems that the Walatkeviczus family must have adopted the surname on that basis.

Among their children they had two known daughters; Alene aka Ellen Mitchell and Grazia aka Grace Mitchell. Their daughter Ellen was born Alene Walatkeviczus on 29 July 1917, during WWI, at 11 Muirpark Rows, Bellshill. The birth was registered by her father Kazis, who signed with his 'x' mark, on 30 July 1917 at the Bellshill Registry Office. Kazis, a coal miner, and his wife Urzula, residing at 116 Main Street, Bellshill, were still alive in December 1938 when their daughter Ellen Mitchell married Billy's father, army physical training instructor James McNeill.

Billy's great-grandparents

Billy's great-grandparents were all born around the mid-19th century. On Billy's paternal line was his great-grandfather James McNeill, a coal miner, who had a son William McNeill (b. ~1876, Paisley) and his great-grandmother Jane McArthur, a jute spinner, who bore her illegitimate daughter Margaret McArthur (b. 19 July 1876, Dundee).

On the Lithuanian maternal lineage was Billy's great-grandfather Mikelaitu Walatkeviczus, a farmer, and his great-grandmother Marie Latikavicz, who bore Kazis Walatkeviczus (b. ~1884, Lithuania). His other great-grandfather was Anton Jurkeniute, also a farmer, and his great-grandmother Agata Jerbulei, who bore Urzula Jurkeniute (b. ~1886, Lithuania).

Chapter 6:

John Clark (left half)

Honours as a Celtic player:

1 European Cup

3 Scottish League titles

3 Scottish Cups

4 Scottish League Cups

The young John Clark

Raised in Chapelhall and Holytown in Lanarkshire, John Clark grew up in a tough working-class environment in a large Catholic family which instilled in him a strong work ethic. Prior to the introduction of the NHS in 1947 - and even into the late 1950s - most children were born at home, but John was an exception to the rule as he was born in hospital. John Patrick Clark was born on 13 March 1941 at the County Hospital, Bellshill to father John Clark, a quarry worker, and mother Elizabeth Doyle. The birth was registered by John's mother Elizabeth on 31 March 1941 at the Bellshill Registry Office.

On the evening of John's birth the Clydeside shipbuilding town of Clydebank was devastated by a German Luftwaffe bombing raid and as baby John ended his second day alive, the Clydebank Blitz continued with a dreadful second night of bombing on the evening of 14 March 1941. As John slept blissfully unaware, the dockland and town of Clydebank was reduced to rubble, just a few miles away on the other side of the River Clyde.

After leaving school John played for the junior side Larkhall Thistle. Ironically, John was raised in the Roman Catholic faith, however, the small Lanarkshire town of Larkhall had a reputation for being staunchly Protestant. A Scotsman news article stated that "green was a colour noticeable for its absence in Larkhall, a small town notable for its Rangers tops and Protestant marching bands". However, John impressed at Larkhall Thistle and he was soon spotted by the Celtic scouts. At the age of 17, Celtic signed him on as a player and he moved to Parkhead in 1958.

In the early years of John's playing career as a wing-half, he showed little sign of his later glory with the Lions. He first attracted attention after scoring the only goal on his debut in a Cup tie replay against Hibernian in 1961. John had been asked to play in place of the injured Celtic legend and captain Bertie Peacock. Unfortunately for Bertie the injury had taken an awful toll and Peacock would not play for Celtic again. They say that one man's misfortune is another man's gain and fate had pushed John's Celtic career onwards.

However, the task of taking over from the great Bertie Peacock would have been difficult for any player. At the outset it was not easy for John, especially as Celtic were mostly underwhelming for much of his early years at the club. In the 1960-61 season John began to make his mark in the first team and towards the end of that season he took over as the regular left half from Billy Price. From 1965 under the guidance of Jock Stein, who developed John into a modern sweeper, his subtle sweeping up in the half-back position beside Billy McNeill was integral to Celtic's ultimate success. In the 1967 final it was Clark and McNeill's pivotal role at the back that allowed Craig and Gemmell the freedom to attack on the overlap and, ultimately, Inter Milan could not cope with Stein's new attacking system.

John's parents – John Clark and Elizabeth Doyle

John Clark was born on 23 October 1913 at Bauchope Street in the coal mining village of Chapelhall, Lanarkshire to father John Clark, a coalminer, and mother Margaret Smith. The birth was registered by John's father John on 25 October 1913 at the Holytown Registry Office. John worked as a quarryman and during WWII he also had a job as an aircraft factory worker helping in the construction of war planes to fight the Luftwaffe. It was here he met his sweetheart Elizabeth Doyle who was working as an aircraft machinist. Elizabeth was born around 1918 to father Michael Doyle, a postman, and mother Bridget Coughlan.

John Clark, 27, an aircraft factory worker, residing at 1 Kennelburn Road, Chapelhall married wife Elizabeth Doyle, 22, an aircraft machinist, residing at 9 Monkland View, Calderbank on 30 November 1940 at St Aloysius, Chapelhall according to the forms of the Roman Catholic Church. The wedding was conducted by Father Thomas Rourke, RC clergyman at St Aloysius; the witnesses were James and Helen

Clark, John's brother and sister, both also of 1 Kennelburn Road. Son John Patrick Clark was born on 13 March 1941 at the County Hospital, Bellshill. The birth was registered by John's mother Elizabeth on 31 March 1941 at the Bellshill Registry Office. At the time of the birth John Clark was employed as a quarry worker.

John's paternal grandparents – John Clark and Margaret Smith

John's paternal grandfather John Clark was born around 1876 in Bothwell, Lanarkshire to father Owen Clark, a blast furnace keeper, and mother Elizabeth Gilmour. In 1881 census John, 5, a scholar, resided at Bent Cottage, Bo'ness Road, Bothwell with his parents and siblings. John's paternal grandmother Margaret Smith was born at 6.45pm two hours before her twin brother James Smith, who arrived at 8.45pm, both on 21 October 1880 in Clarkston, New Monkland, Lanarkshire to father Bernard Smith, a stone mason dresser, and mother Ellen McGowan. The births were actually registered by the twin babies' great-grandmother Ann Everett, who signed with her 'x' mark, on 6 November 1880 at the New Monkland Registry Office.

In the Victorian era New Monkland was the parish which is now effectively surrounding the town of Airdrie. By the turn of the 20th century, John and Margaret were both living and working in Airdrie, Lanarkshire when they married. John was living at Briton's Land in the mining village of Chapelhall beside Airdrie. The word 'land' in this context actually is an old Scots term for a tenement building and Mr Briton would have been the landlord or proprietor of the building.

John Clark, 24, a coal miner, residing at Briton's Land, Chapelhall by Airdrie married wife Margaret Smith, 19, a paper mill worker, residing at 117 Forrest Street, Airdrie on 28 September 1900 at St Margaret's Church, Airdrie according to the forms of the Roman Catholic Church. The wedding was conducted by the exotically named Father Stubart van Stiphout, Catholic clergyman; the best man was James Clark, John's brother, and the best maid was Bridget Smith, Margaret's sister. John and Margaret had three known children; John, James and Helen.

Their son John Clark was born on 23 October 1913 at Bauchope Street in the coal mining village of Chapelhall, Lanarkshire. The birth was registered by John's father John on 25 October 1913 at the Holytown Registry Office. John, a coal miner, was dead by 1940 as his wife Margaret was a widow when their son John Clark married wife Elizabeth Doyle.

John's maternal grandparents – Michael Doyle and Bridget Coughlan

John's maternal grandfather Michael Doyle and his maternal grandmother Bridget Coughlan have not been researched in detail, but suffice to say, given their surnames, they are almost certainly descended from Irish stock. Michael Doyle, a postman, and his wife Bridget had a daughter Elizabeth Doyle (b. ~1918). Michael Doyle, a postman, was dead by 1940 and his wife Bridget was a widow by then living in Calderbank, Lanarkshire.

John's great-grandparents

On John's paternal line his great-grandfather Owen Clark, a blast furnace keeper in an iron and steel works, was born around 1835 in Ireland and his great-grandmother Elizabeth Gilmour was born around 1845 in Bothwell, Lanarkshire. Owen and Elizabeth had six known children including son John (b. ~1876, Bothwell). In 1881 census Owen Clark, 46, a furnace keeper, resided at Bent Cottage, Bothwell with wife Elizabeth, 36, children Mary, 16, a mill worker, James, 15, a coal miner, then Catherine, 13, Roseann, 11, John, 5, all at school, and baby Sarah, 3. By the turn of the 20th century, Owen, a blast furnace keeper, and his wife Elizabeth were both dead.

John's other paternal great-grandfather was Bernard Smith, a stone mason dresser, and his great-grandmother was Helen McGowan, aka Ellen, and they were both born around the mid-19th century. Bernard and Ellen had three known children; twins Margaret and James and daughter Bridget. Margaret was born at 6.45pm, two hours before her twin brother James, who arrived at 8.45pm, both on 21 October 1880 in Clarkston, New Monkland, Lanarkshire to father Bernard and mother Ellen. By the turn of the 20th century both Bernard, a causeway dresser, and his wife Ellen were both dead.

John's great-great-great-grandmother

John Clark's great-great-grandparents have not been specifically researched for this book, however, one of his great-great-great-grandmothers turned up in the research. When John's great-grandmother Margaret Smith and her twin brother James were both born on 21 October 1880 in the coal mining village of Clarkston by Airdrie, the births were registered by their great-grandmother Ann Everett on 6 November 1880 at the New Monkland Registry Office. Ann Everett was John Clark's great-great-great-grandmother, who was most likely born in Ireland in the early 19th century. Like many elderly people in the late 19th century who had gained little or no formal education Ann could not read or write. Ann signed with her 'x' mark when she registered Margaret and James's births in 1880.

Chapter 7

Jimmy Johnstone (outside right)

Honours as a Celtic player:

1 European Cup

9 Scottish League titles

4 Scottish Cups

5 Scottish League Cups

The young Jimmy Johnstone

In 2002 Jimmy Johnstone was voted by Celtic supporters as the greatest ever Celtic player to have worn the green and white hoops. The author watched 'wee Jinky' on many occasions while spectating from the old Jungle stand at Parkhead, mainly towards the latter end of his career at Celtic, and what Jimmy could do with a football was magical at times. Personally speaking, the author's own favourite Hoops player was Kenny Dalglish, but it is difficult to argue with the 'greatest ever' accolade received by that lovable wee rogue Johnstone. Jimmy's off-field antics were as legendary as those on the pitch. For instance, the rowing boat fiasco at Largs has gone down in the annals of footballing folklore.

Jimmy was the youngest of five surviving children of a family of eight. Tragically, three of his siblings died in infancy. He had an older brother Patrick and sisters Theresa, Ann and

Mary. As the war in Europe raged on, the Allies pushed the Nazis back in France and on the same day that the Germans surrendered in Calais, James Connelly Johnstone was born on 30 September 1944 at 647 Old Edinburgh Road, Viewpark to father Matthew Johnstone, a coal miner brusher, and mother Sarah Crawley. The birth was registered by Jimmy's father Matthew on 4 October 1944 at the Uddingston Registry Office.

Jimmy stated that he had been kicking a ball for as long as he could remember. From a very early age, he spent hours playing in streets and public parks, sometimes alone, sometimes with groups of friends and occasionally with his older brother Pat. Pat was a fine player himself and Celtic were rumoured to be watching him closely. Unfortunately, he was badly injured playing for his local boys' guild team and the resultant cartilage damage effectively ended his career. Years later Jimmy stated in his autobiography that he could remember the disappointment on his father Matt's face when Pat suffered the injury.

Jimmy's footballing talent was first discovered at just eight years old by his schoolteacher John Crines. Mr Crines eventually persuaded the shy Jimmy to join the school team St Columba's Primary in Viewpark. With Jimmy in the team, St Columba's became almost unstoppable and won every competition the school entered. Jimmy then attended St John's Secondary School in Uddingston and helped his school team to previously unheard of success.

During a St John's school trip to Manchester to play in a tournament, Jimmy had the chance to watch his footballing hero, Sir Stanley Matthews. Jimmy was in awe of Matthews' ability with a ball. He would spend hours copying the techniques Matthews had used in his early years to perfect his ball skills, particularly the trademark dribbling that Johnstone became world-renowned for. Jimmy had actually been spotted by Manchester United scouts when he played there and he had been brought to the attention of Matt Busby.

Fortunately for Johnstone - and Celtic - Frank Cairney, the chaplain of St John's, and an ardent Celtic supporter, threw United off the scent. Father Cairney told Celtic scout John Higgins of United's interest and Jimmy was invited to train with the Parkhead club two nights a week. In October 1961 Jimmy made his debut for the reserves against St Johnstone in a 4-2 win. Jimmy scored one and made the other three. Watching the game was then Celtic manager Jimmy McGrory who signed Jimmy Johnstone and Tommy Gemmell together on that same night. Jimmy was farmed out to the junior club Blantyre Celtic to hone his skills. This was supposed to be for a year but such was his ability that Jimmy was soon chosen to play at junior level for Scotland against Northern Ireland. Celtic scout Jimmy Gribben was watching the game and immediately suggested to McGrory that Jimmy be recalled to Celtic.

Jimmy's career really came to the fore when Jock Stein arrived in 1965. Their tumultuous on-off relationship was as legendary as their footballing careers. Jock Stein was like a frustrated father to a mischievous son, but Stein was unequivocal about Johnstone's ability. Stein had guided Celtic to victory in the European Cup and he led the Hoops to the famous nine in a row League Championships. However, in the Daily Telegraph, Stein famously stated, "I would like to be remembered for keeping the wee man, Jimmy Johnstone, in the game five years longer than he might have been. That is my greatest achievement."

Jimmy's parents – Matthew Johnstone and Sarah Crawley

Matthew Johnstone, aka Matt, was born on 9 July 1903 at Oilwork Row, Aitkenhead, Bothwell, Lanarkshire to father Matthew Johnstone, a brusher in a coal pit, and mother Theresa McDiarmid (or McDermott). The birth was registered by Matthew's father Matthew, who signed with his 'x' mark, on 4 August 1903 at the Uddingston Registry Office.

After leaving school Matthew went down the coal mines like his father before him. Jimmy's mother Sarah was also born in the same village as Jimmy's father Matt and they were likely childhood sweethearts. It is also likely that their love blossomed at the local colliery as both of them worked there, although, by the 1920s, the Johnstone family had moved from the village of Aitkenhead to the nearby village of Tannochside.

The coal mines are long gone from Tannochside and the main industry there is the Tunnock's chocolate confectionery factory; famous for its caramel wafers, caramel logs and chocolate teacakes. The managing director, Boyd Tunnock, nicknamed the 'Willy Wonka of Tannochside', went to the same Glasgow school that the author attended, Allan Glen's.

It might be difficult nowadays to imagine that into the 20th century young girls like Sarah were still working at the pithead, but females were regularly employed in cleaning coal and picking out the dross. Sarah Crawley was born on 6 October 1905 at 40 Old Rows, Aitkenhead, Bothwell, Lanarkshire to father Patrick Crawley, a colliery stoker, and mother Catherine Devlin. The birth was registered by Sarah's father Patrick on 26 October 1905 at the Uddingston Registry Office.

Matthew Johnstone, 23, a coal miner, residing at 85 Cuthbert Street, Tannochside married wife Sarah Crawley, 20, a pithead worker, residing at 11 Oilwork Row, Aitkenhead, Bothwell on 23 September 1926 at St John the Baptist's Church, Uddingston according to the forms of the Roman Catholic Church. The wedding was conducted by Father Daniel O'Brien, RC clergyman in Uddingston; the best man was James Dougan, of 16 Oilwork Row, Aitkenhead and the best maid was Mary Johnstone, Matt's sister, of 85 Cuthbert Street, Tannochside.

Matt and Sarah had eight known children, although tragically three of them died in infancy. Prior to the introduction of the National Health Service in 1947 infant mortality was still an all too common feature in the large families of the poor working class, and losing three children out of eight must have been a terrible loss to Jimmy's parents. The surviving five children were Patrick, aka Pat, daughters Theresa, Ann, Mary and their youngest son Jimmy. By the outset of WWII the family were living in Viewpark, Uddingston. Son James Connelly Johnstone was born on 30 September 1944 at 647 Old Edinburgh Road, Viewpark. The birth was registered by Jimmy's father Matthew on 4 October 1944 at the Uddingston Registry Office.

Jimmy's paternal grandparents – Matthew Johnstone and Theresa McDiarmid

Jimmy's paternal grandfather Matthew Johnstone was born around 1866 to father also Matthew Johnstone, a labourer, and mother Ann Murray. Jimmy's paternal grandmother Theresa McDiarmid was born on 11 March 1866 at 33 Back-causeway, Westmuir, Glasgow to father Neil McDiarmid, a coal miner, and mother Margaret McNulty. The birth was registered by Theresa's father Neil McDiarmid, who signed with his 'x' mark, a few days later in March 1866 at the Glasgow Registry Office. Westmuir was a colliery village in Shettleston which lay to the east of Glasgow in those days.

Like all Gaelic surnames the spelling of Theresa's surname, which became McDiarmid, was usually down to the registrar's own interpretation. At her wedding Theresa, who could write unlike her husband Matthew, signed her name as McDermott. Recorded also as MacDermot, MacDermott, McDermot, McDermott, and Dermot - this is a famous royal and noble Irish surname. It is a patronymic with the clan claiming descent from Dermot, the King of Connacht in the 12th century. The Gaelic prefix 'mac' means 'son of' followed by the personal name Diarmuid (later Dermot) meaning 'free man'.

Theresa was Matthew Johnstone's second wife. By 1899 Matthew was a widower and it is possible that he had children from his first marriage. Matthew Johnstone, 33, a coal miner, residing at 37 Longmuir, Drumpark, Old Monkland married wife Theresa McDermott, 32, a domestic servant, residing at Quarry Row, Braehead, Old Monkland on 14 July 1899 at the RC Church, Baillieston according to the forms of the Roman Catholic Church. The wedding was conducted by Father Peter H Terken, Catholic clergyman; the best man was Edward McDermott, Theresa's brother and the best maid was Mary Greer.

Matthew and Theresa's son Matthew Johnstone was born on 9 July 1903 at Oilwork Row, Aitkenhead, Bothwell, Lanarkshire. The birth was registered by Matthew's father Matthew, who signed with his 'x' mark, on 4 August 1903 at the Uddingston Registry Office. Matthew, a coal miner, was dead by 1926 and Theresa was a widow when their son Matt married Sarah Crawley.

Jimmy's maternal grandparents – Patrick Crawley and Catherine Devlin

Jimmy's maternal grandfather Patrick Crawley and his maternal grandmother Catherine Devlin were both born around 1875 in Ireland most likely in the northern province of Ulster. Patrick Crawley married wife Catherine Devlin on 26 January 1901 in Belfast, County Antrim, but by 1905 they had immigrated to live and work in the tough Lanarkshire coalfields, where they had daughter Sarah. Daughter Sarah Crawley was born on 6 October 1905 at 40 Old Rows, Aitkenhead, Bothwell, Lanarkshire. The birth was registered by Sarah's father Patrick on 26 October 1905 at the Uddingston Registry Office. Patrick, a colliery stoker, and his wife Catherine were both still alive in 1926 when their daughter Sarah married Matt Johnstone.

Jimmy's great-grandparents

On Jimmy's paternal line was his great-grandfather Matthew Johnstone, a labourer, and his great-grandmother was Ann Murray and they had a son Matthew (b. ~1866). By the end of the 19th century both Matthew, a labourer, and Ann were still alive.

Jimmy's other paternal great-grandfather was Neil McDiarmid (or McDermott) who was born around 1840 to father Patrick McDiarmid and mother Mary Hartie. Jimmy's great-grandmother was Margaret McNulty (or McInulty) who was born around 1838 to father Edward McInulty, a tailor, and mother Helen Leitch. By 1865 Neil McDiarmid was likely to be a coal miner at the R. Gray & Company mine at Westmuir Colliery in Shettleston and living at Westmuir Street in Parkhead.

This was still twelve years before Brother Walfrid called the foundation meeting of the Celtic Football Club at St Mary's Chapel, where coincidentally Neil and Margaret were to be married, and Neil would remain unaware that his descendant Jimmy Johnstone would become the greatest ever Celtic player over a century later.

Neil McDiarmid, 25, a coal miner, residing at 80 Westmuir Street, Parkhead, Glasgow married wife Margaret McInulty, 27, a factory worker, residing at 37 Colliers Row, Glasgow on 12 June 1865 at St Mary's Chapel, Calton, Glasgow according to the forms of the Roman Catholic Church. The wedding was conducted by Father E Noonan; the witnesses were Robert and Theresa McInulty, likely to be Margaret's brother and sister.

Neil and Margaret had two known children; son Edward and daughter Theresa. Daughter Theresa McDiarmid was born on 11 March 1866 at 33 Backcauseway, Westmuir, Glasgow. The birth was registered by Theresa's father Neil, who signed with his 'x' mark, a few days later in March 1866 at the Glasgow Registry Office. By the end of the 19th century Neil McDiarmid, a coal miner, was a widower as his wife Margaret was dead.

Jimmy's great-great-grandparents

Continuing down Jimmy's maternal line his great-great-grandfather was Patrick McDiarmid, a labourer, and his great-great-grandmother was Mary Hartie and they had a son Neil (b. ~1840). Patrick and Mary were born in the early years of the 19th century and were almost certainly Irish. Patrick McDiarmid, a labourer, was dead by 1865 and his wife Mary was a widow by then.

Still on the maternal line, his other great-great-grandfather was Edward McInulty, a tailor, and his great-great-grandmother was Helen Leitch and they had three known children; son Robert and daughters Margaret (b. ~1838) and Theresa. Edward and Helen were also born in the early years of the 19th century and again they were almost certainly of Irish extraction. Edward McInulty, a tailor, was a widower by 1865 and his wife Helen was dead by then.

Chapter 8

Willie Wallace (inside right)

Honours as a Celtic player:

1 European Cup

5 Scottish League titles

3 Scottish Cups

2 Scottish League Cups

The young Willie Wallace

Willie Wallace was known as 'Wispy' to his teammates, because of his quiet voice and his forename initials of W.S.B., which he inherited from his maternal grandfather. Just over a fortnight after one of Britain's lowest ebbs in WWII, the humiliating but ultimately heroic retreat from France following the Battle of Dunkirk, Willie was born in Kirkintilloch. William Semple Brown Wallace was born on 23 June 1940 at 39 Hillhead, Kirkintilloch, Dunbartonshire to father Andrew Wallace, an iron dresser, and mother Sarah White McLellan Brown. The birth was registered by Willie's father Andrew on the following day 24 June 1940 at the Kirkintilloch Registry Office.

Willie began his senior football career with Stirlingshire side Stenhousemuir in 1958 and then he moved to Raith Rovers in Kirkcaldy, Fife in October 1959. He soon attracted the attention of Heart of Midlothian, and he joined the successful Tynecastle club in 1961. Willie spent five full seasons in Edinburgh with Hearts, winning a League Cup winner's medal in October 1962 as Hearts beat Kilmarnock 1-0 in the final. He was in the Hearts team that lost the league on goal average to Kilmarnock in 1965. Willie won seven caps for Scotland. He faced England in two memorable Home International matches; England won 4-3 at Hampden in 1966, with England going on to win the World Cup that summer, and the following year Scotland won 3-2 at Wembley against the World Champions in 1967.

Willie made it known that he was keen to move away from Hearts and the Glasgow Rangers were known to be interested. However, on 6 December 1966 with Rangers in Germany on European Cup Winners Cup duties, Jock Stein struck and Willie signed for Celtic for a club record at that time of £30,000. In retrospect, when looking at the modern era where clubs like Barcelona, Real Madrid, Bayern Munich, Manchester United and Chelsea spend multi-millions every year seeking glory in the Champions League, the enormity of what Stein achieved cannot be underestimated.

Willie Wallace was the only major signing that Stein made in the 1966-67 season in which to finally construct the Lisbon Lions team. All the rest were home-grown boys who joined Celtic in the main from the amateur and junior ranks, apart from Joe McBride who Stein signed the previous season from Motherwell for £22,000 in 1965.

Willie's parents – Andrew Wallace and Sarah White McLellan Brown

Andrew Wallace was born on 5 September 1909 at 3 Shamrock Street in the small town of Kirkintilloch, Dunbartonshire to father James Wallace, an iron dresser, and mother Catherine Glen. The birth was registered by Andrew's father James on 27 September 1909 at the Kirkintilloch Registry Office. Andrew followed his father into the iron works and he too worked as an iron dresser. Sarah White McLellan Brown was born the previous month on 1 August 1909 at 3 Red Brae Road, Kirkintilloch to father William Semple Brown, a canal boatman, and mother Margaret McLellan. The birth was registered by Sarah's mother Margaret Brown on 23 August 1909 at the Kirkintilloch Registry Office.

Andrew Wallace, 25, an iron dresser, residing at 14 Donaldson Street, Kirkintilloch married wife Sarah White McLellan Brown, 25, a slag wool worker, residing at 18 Hillhead, Kirkintilloch on 26 October 1934 at nearby 18 Hillhead, Kirkintilloch according to the forms of the Church of Scotland. The wedding was conducted by Rev J Angus Morrison, minister of Kirkintilloch; the best man was Hugh Wallace, Andrew's brother, and the best maid was Margaret Brown, Sarah's sister. Son William was born on 23 June 1940 at 39 Hillhead, Kirkintilloch. The birth was registered by Willie's father Andrew on the following day 24 June 1940 at the Kirkintilloch Registry Office.

Willie's paternal grandparents – James Wallace and Catherine Glen

Willie's paternal grandfather James Wallace was born around 1873 in Kirkintilloch, Dunbartonshire to father Andrew

Wallace, a general labourer, and mother Mary Tonner, aka Marian. In 1881 census James, 18, an iron dresser resided at 109 Townhead Street, Kirkintilloch with his parents and siblings. Willie's paternal grandmother Catherine Glen was born around 1878 to father Hugh Glen, a cotton weaver, and mother Mary McBlane.

James Wallace, 31, an iron dresser, residing at 112 Townhead, Kirkintilloch married wife Catherine Glen, 28, a domestic servant, residing at 39 Union Street, Kirkintilloch on 13 July 1906 in the Temperance Hall, Kirkintilloch according to the forms of the Church of Scotland. The wedding was conducted by Rev Andrew Armit, minister of Monikie in Forfarshire; the best man was David Irvine and the best maid was Jane Glen, Catherine's sister.

James and Catherine had two known sons; Andrew and Hugh. Son Andrew Wallace was born on 5 September 1909 at 3 Shamrock Street in Kirkintilloch. The birth was registered by Andrew's father James on 27 September 1909 at the Kirkintilloch Registry Office. James, an iron dresser, was dead by 1934 as his wife Catherine was a widow when their son Andrew married wife Sarah.

Willie's maternal grandparents – William Semple Brown and Margaret McLellan

Willie Wallace was named in honour of his maternal grandfather William Semple Brown and from whose initials Willie's nickname of 'Wispy' originated. William Semple Brown was born around 1884 to father Francis Brown, a boatman, and mother Janet Semple. After leaving school William became a coal miner but later he became a canal boatman, like his father Francis, in Kirkintilloch on the Forth and Clyde Canal.

Prior to the introduction of the railways in the 1830s the Forth and Clyde Canal was the main transportation artery for the Central Belt of Scotland, although by the 1880s its importance for transporting mainly coal and freight goods was waning. Kirkintilloch was once a key port on the canal between Port Dundas, Glasgow and Falkirk, where the Forth and Clyde canal linked with the Union Canal for onward traffic to Edinburgh.

Willie's maternal grandmother Margaret McLellan, aka Maggie, was born around 1885 to father James McLellan, a mason journeyman, and mother Agnes Stirling. After leaving school Maggie became a power loom weaver in the weaving village of Pollokshaws, Eastwood, Renfrewshire, making her one of the 'queer folk o' the Shaws'.

The weaving history of Pollokshaws goes back to the 15th century when at that time the finest weavers were the Flemish from Flanders in Belgium. They were encouraged to come over to settle in Scotland to bring their weaving skills and it is believed some settled in Pollokshaws village on the lands of the Maxwells of Pollok. The legend was that, because they spoke for generations in a foreign tongue, they were given the moniker of the 'queer folk of the Shaws'. The reader will recall from the preface, that on that famous night of 25 May 1967, the author watched the European Cup final at his gran and grandfather's high rise flat in Pollokshaws, more than 80 years after Maggie's birth.

William Semple Brown, 22, a coal miner, residing at 22 Salton Place, Kirkintilloch married wife Maggie McLellan,

21, a power loom weaver, residing at 16 College Street, Pollok-shaws on 27 April 1906 at Maggie's home according to the forms of the Church of Scotland. The wedding was conducted by Rev James Mackie; the best man was Lauchlan Cumming and the best maid was Sarah White McLellan, Maggie's sister. Daughter Sarah White McLellan Brown was born on 1 August 1909 at 3 Red Brae Road, Kirkintilloch. The birth was registered by Sarah's mother Margaret on 23 August 1909 at the Kirkintilloch Registry Office. William Brown, a widowed canal boatman, was still alive in 1934 and his wife Maggie was dead by that time.

Willie's great-grandparents

On Willie's paternal line his great-grandfather Andrew Wallace, a general labourer, was born around 1838 in Glasgow and his great-grandmother Mary Tonner, aka Marian, was born around 1843 in Kirkintilloch. Andrew and Mary had three known children including son James (b. ~1873, Kirkintilloch). In 1891 census Andrew Wallace, 53, an iron foundry labourer, resided at 109 Townhead Street, Kirkintilloch with wife Marian, 48, children Andrew, 21, an iron moulder, James, 18, an iron dresser, and Maggie H, 13, a scholar. By 1906 Andrew Wallace, a general labourer living in Townhead, Kirkintilloch, was a widower and his wife Mary was dead. Willie's other paternal great-grandfather was Hugh Glen, a cotton weaver, and his great-grandmother was Mary McBlane. They had two known daughters Catherine

(b. ~1878) and Jane. By 1906 Hugh Glen, a cotton weaver, was dead and his wife Mary was a widow.

On Willie's maternal line was his great-grandfather Francis Brown, a boatman on the Forth and Clyde Canal, and his great-grandmother Janet Semple and they had a son William Semple Brown (b. ~1884). In 1906 when son William married wife Maggie, Francis, a canal boatman, and Janet were living at 22 Salton Place, Kirkintilloch, Dunbartonshire. Willie's other maternal great-grandfather was James McLellan, a mason journeyman, and his great-grandmother was Agnes Stirling. James and Agnes had two known daughters Margaret, aka Maggie, (b. ~1885) and Sarah White McLellan. In 1906 James, a stone mason, and Agnes were living at 16 College Street, Pollokshaws, Eastwood, Renfrewshire.

Between 1983 and 1995 the author lived in Parkhill Road in Pollokshaws in a red-sandstone terrace house built by the Stirling-Maxwell family of Pollok Estate for their tenants in 1908. It would be nice to think that James McLellan was one of the jobbing stone masons who built the author's home in Parkhill Road.

In fact, the author's family history is also very much associated with stone masonry in Pollokshaws. His own great-grandfather Thomas McCue was born in 1876 at 200 St. James Street (now called Seaward Street), Kinning Park, Govan to Irish Catholic parents Thomas and Mary. That must have been too close for comfort to the newly formed Ibrox team - Glasgow Rangers.

In the 1881 census, Thomas, age 3, had moved with his parents to live at 16 Pleasance Street, Pollokshaws. Thirty years later in 1911 census Thomas, 35, resided at 16 Coustonhill Street, Pollokshaws and he was working as a stone mason's labourer. It is likely Thomas McCue would have known James McLellan, Willie's great-grandfather. Who knows, they may even have worked together. The following year in 1912 the suburban village of Pollokshaws was subsumed into the expanding conurbation of the city of Glasgow. The author's 136 year family connection to the 'queer folk o' the Shaws' continues to this day and his sister Jess still lives at the Wellgreen in Pollokshaws.

Chapter 9

Stevie Chalmers (centre forward)

Honours as a Celtic player:
1 European Cup
4 Scottish League titles
3 Scottish Cups
4 Scottish League Cups

The young Stevie Chalmers

The great Stevie Chalmers will forever be remembered as the man who scored the most important goal in the history of Celtic. With only seven minutes remaining, the talented centre-forward deftly guided Bobby Murdoch's fierce shot into the back of the net to claim the winner in that 1967 European Cup final against Inter Milan in Lisbon. That defining moment ensured Stevie and his team-mates would be immortalised as Lisbon Lions. Stevie was raised in the Celtic stronghold of the Garngad, Glasgow, as was that other famous Celtic son, Jimmy McGrory.

Thomas Stephen Chalmers, aka Stevie, was born on Boxing Day 26 December 1935 at the Maternity Hospital, Rottenrow, Glasgow to father David Chalmers, a power company's labourer, and mother Margaret Nevins. The birth was registered by Stevie's father David at the Glasgow Registry Office.

At the time the family were living at 56 James Nisbet Street, Roystonhill, Glasgow in the Garngad.

In the early 20th century the area was still known by its original historic name of the Garngad, derived from the Gaelic word 'garn' meaning rough ground surrounding the Gad burn, which ran through the district. It was home to a high proportion of Irish Catholic immigrants who gained employment in the gas, chemical, iron and steel and railway works in the adjacent districts of Provan, St Rollox and Springburn. However, during the era of the Great Depression in the 1920s and 1930s, which earned Glasgow its 'No Mean City' label of slums, drunkenness, violence and razor gangs, the reputation of the Garngad became deeply tarnished. It landed itself with the Glasgow rhyming slang nickname of 'The Garngad - the Good and the Bad'.

The City Fathers in their wisdom decided in 1942 to rename the area Royston, after the legendary Rob Roy MacGregor, who once lived there in the early 18th century. This was followed by a programme of slum clearance and housing redevelopment in the early 1950s. However, the historic name of the Garngad still fondly persists with the local inhabitants even into the 21st century and the local public house on Royston Road retains the name - 'The Garngad'.

As a boy Stevie had played at junior international level for Scotland and he joined Celtic in February 1959 from Ashfield Juniors at the age of 23. He became one of 'Kelly's Kids' along with other greats such as Jimmy Johnstone, Billy McNeill, John Hughes and Tommy Gemmell. However, playing in a Celtic side packed with ability, but lacking real guidance, Stevie found the quest for silverware to be a fruitless and frustrating task.

All that would change in the most dramatic fashion with the arrival of the legendary Jock Stein as manager in 1965. Stevie Chalmers was set on the path to that dramatic 83rd minute goal in the Estádio Nacional and his place in Celtic folklore.

Stevie's parents – David Chalmers and Margaret Nevins

David Chalmers was born on 27 June 1897 at 61 Quarry Street, Hamilton, Lanarkshire to father David Chalmers, a tinsmith journeyman, and mother Mary Hunter. The birth was registered by his father David on 2 July 1897 at the Hamilton Registry Office. David was raised in the Protestant faith in Hamilton, although he later converted to Catholicism and raised his family as Catholic. As a young man, many years before Stevie's breakthrough at Parkhead, David Chalmers had tried unsuccessfully to make it at Celtic. He later moved down the River Clyde to play for the lower division club Clydebank. His son Stevie's success at Celtic more than made up for David's lost chance and it must have been a source of great pride to see Stevie in the green and white hoops.

The year after David's birth Stevie's mother Margaret Nevins (or Nevans) was also born in Hamilton. Margaret Nevans was born on 8 January 1898 at 4 Young Street, Hamilton to father Thomas Nevans, a railway platelayer, and mother Elizabeth Conway. The birth was registered by Margaret's father Thomas on 7 February 1898 at the Hamilton Registry Office. Margaret was raised in the Roman Catholic faith in Hamilton.

David Chalmers, 24, an iron moulder journeyman, residing at 108 Burnbank Road, Hamilton married wife Margaret Nevans, 23, a baker's assistant, residing at 4 Back Row, Hamilton on 9 September 1921 at the RC Chapel, Hamilton according to the forms of the Roman Catholic Church. The wedding was conducted by Father William McAvoy; the best man was Charles J Kelly and the best maid was Elizabeth Murray. By the 1930s David and Margaret had moved to live and work in the Garngad district of Glasgow.

Their son Thomas Stephen Chalmers was born on Boxing Day, 26 December 1935, at the Maternity Hospital, Rottenrow, Glasgow. The birth was registered by Stevie's father David, then employed as a power company's labourer, at the Glasgow Registry Office. At the time the family were living at 56 James Nisbet Street, Roystonhill, Glasgow.

Stevie's paternal grandparents – David Chalmers and Mary Love Hunter

Stevie's paternal grandfather David Chalmers was born around 1864 in Hamilton, Lanarkshire to father David Chalmers, a master tinsmith, and mother Jane Welsh. In 1871 census David, 7, a scholar, resided at No.16 Low Patrick Street, Hamilton with his parents and his many siblings. After leaving school David apprenticed as a tinsmith with his father and by the 1890s the family were living at 61 Campbell Street, Hamilton not far from the Hunter family who lived at 1 Bothwell Road, Hamilton. Stevie's paternal grandmother Mary Love Hunter was born around 1870 to father William

Hunter, a spirit merchant, and mother Margaret Campbell Wood.

David Chalmers, 30, a tinsmith journeyman, residing at 61 Campbell Street, Hamilton married wife Mary Love Hunter, 24, residing at 1 Bothwell Road, Hamilton on 3 October 1894 at Mary's home according to the forms of the Church of Scotland. The wedding was conducted by Rev E L Thomson, 2nd charge minister of Hamilton; the best man was Robert Hetherington and the best maid was Eliza McLaren. David and Mary had a known son also David Chalmers. Son David Chalmers was born on 27 June 1897 at 61 Quarry Street, Hamilton, Lanarkshire. The birth was registered by his father David on 2 July 1897 at the Hamilton Registry Office. By 1921 David Chalmers was still alive and working as a colliery lamp man and his wife Mary was still living then too.

Stevie's maternal grandparents – Thomas Nevans and Elizabeth Conway

Stevie Chalmers was named in honour of his maternal grandfather Thomas Nevans (or Nevins), although he was never widely known as Thomas. Stevie confirmed that his forename was actually Thomas to Kerrydale Street Celtic Wiki member 'CaltonBhoy1967' who asked Stevie about it personally at the 2-1 victory over Motherwell at Celtic Park on 13 April 2010.

Thomas Nevans was born around 1845 to father Michael Nevans, a labourer, and mother Agnes Trainer. Stevie's maternal grandmother Elizabeth Conway, aka Eliza, was born around 1855 to father Thomas Conway, a coal miner, and mother Catherine Murphy. Thomas Nevans, 26, a coal miner, married wife Eliza Conway, just sweet 16, a power loom weaver, both residing at 49 Ruchlee Street, Hamilton on 1 June 1871 at the RC Chapel in Hamilton according to the forms of the Roman Catholic Church. The wedding was conducted by Father James Danaher, RC clergyman; the best man was James Hand and the best maid was Catherine Murphy. Thomas and Elizabeth had eight known children in Hamilton including daughter Margaret (b. 8 January 1898).

By 1891 Thomas was working as a railway platelayer in Hamilton, which suggests he would almost certainly have been employed by the Caledonian Railway Company at that time, although it appears he may have returned later to work in the coal mines. In 1891 census Thomas Nevans, 45, a railway platelayer, resided at 4 Young Street, Hamilton with wife Elizabeth, 35, children Thomas, 18, an iron moulder, then Joseph, 13, John, 11, Mary, 6, all scholars, William, 4, Teresa, 3, and baby Agnes, 1. Their daughter Margaret Nevans was born on 8 January 1898 at 4 Young Street, Hamilton. The birth was registered by Margaret's father Thomas on 7 February 1898 at the Hamilton Registry Office. Thomas Nevans, a coal miner, was dead by 1921 and his wife Elizabeth was a widow by that time.

Stevie's great-grandparents
Stevie's great-grandparents were all born about the 1830s. On Stevie's paternal line his great-grandfather David Chalmers, a master tinsmith, was born around 1838. His great-grand-

mother Jane Welsh was born around 1836 both in Hamilton, Lanarkshire and the couple had eight known children including son David (b. ~1864, Hamilton). In 1871 census David Chalmers, 33, a tinsmith, resided at No.16 Low Patrick Street, Hamilton with wife Jane, 35, children William, 15, a tinsmith, then John, 11, Isabella, 9, David, 7, all at school, Catherine, 5, Elizabeth, 3, James, 2, and baby Thomas, just 1 month old. By the mid-1890s David Chalmers, a master tinsmith living in Hamilton, and his wife Jane were still alive.

Stevie's other paternal great-grandfather was William Hunter, a spirit merchant, and his great-grandmother was Margaret Campbell Wood and they had a daughter Mary Love Hunter (b. ~1870). By the mid-1890s William Hunter was widowed and still working as a spirit merchant in Hamilton. His wife Margaret was dead by then.

On his maternal line was his great-grandfather Michael Nevans, a labourer, and his great-grandmother was Agnes Trainer. They had a son Thomas (b. ~1845). By 1871 Michael Nevans, a labourer, and his wife Agnes were both dead. Stevie's other maternal great-grandfather was Thomas Conway, a coal miner, and his great-grandmother was Catherine Murphy and they had a daughter Elizabeth, aka Eliza, (b. ~1855). By 1871 Thomas Conway, a coal miner, was dead and his wife Catherine was a widow. It is almost certain that the Nevans, Trainer, Conway and Murphy lines are all descended from Irish Catholic ancestry.

Chapter 10

Bertie Auld (inside left)

Honours as a Celtic player:
1 European Cup
6 Scottish League titles
4 Scottish Cups
5 Scottish League Cups

The young Bertie Auld

Bertie Auld's mother Margaret was the daughter of a fish and fruit merchant in the seaside town of Girvan in Ayrshire. In the late 1920s she would rise before seven in the morning, load up her father's horse and cart and go out to sell her produce come rain, hail, or shine. Her name was Margaret Diamond Devlin. One day a young unemployed Glaswegian turned up in Girvan looking for work. Joe Auld got the job from Bertie's maternal grandfather and he won Margaret's hand in marriage. Bertie's mother was a Roman Catholic and his father was a Protestant.

Robert Auld was born on 23 March 1938 at 95 Panmure Street, Maryhill, Glasgow to father John Lambie Auld, a builder's labourer, and mother Margaret Diamond Devlin. The birth was registered by Bertie's father John L Auld on 28 March 1938 at the Glasgow Registry Office. Bertie was raised in the Protestant faith, but bigotry never entered into the Auld household. Although WWII broke out just a year and a half after his birth, the young Bertie only had vague memories of the sirens and of hearing the Clydebank Blitz in March 1941.

Bertie attended Springbank Primary School and his main hobby was kicking a ball about the streets until it was dark. Many evenings were spent playing football in Ruchill Park with his mates. Bertie continued his education at East Park Secondary School. His top subject was woodwork, but all Bertie wanted to be when he grew up was to play as a professional footballer. When he left school at 15, he joined Halliday's the butcher before becoming a joiner. When he was not working as a joiner, he played amateur with Panmure Thistle. Bertie was then spotted by the Scottish Junior side Maryhill Harp, but it was not long before he was scouted by Celtic in 1955.

Bertie and his dad Joe were driven from Panmure Street to Celtic Park in a neighbour John McNellis's old Austin car to meet the legendary Celtic manager Jimmy McGrory. McGrory offered the young 16 year old Bertie a £20 signing on fee and £2 a week in wages. Both Clyde and Partick Thistle had offered Bertie more money, but Joe Auld accepted Celtic's offer without question and another Lisbon Lion was in the making.

Bertie's parents – John Lambie Auld and Margaret Diamond Devlin

John Lambie Auld, aka Joe, was born on 27 August 1904 at 69 Harvie Street, Bridgeton, Glasgow to father Robert

Auld, a machinery beltmaker, and mother Elizabeth Stewart. The birth was registered by Joe's mother Elizabeth on 13 September 1904 at the Glasgow Registry Office. After leaving school Joe became an electrician's labourer to trade. As Bertie detailed in his autobiography, Joe had been travelling across Ayrshire during the era of the Great Depression in the early 1930s. Joe had found a job at Harry Devlin's general store in Girvan where he met his sweetheart Margaret, who worked long hours in her father's business.

Bertie's mother Margaret Diamond Devlin was born on St Andrew's Day, 30 November 1907, at 27 Glendowne Street, Girvan to father Henry Devlin, a fish dealer, and mother Wilhelmina McCrae. The birth was registered by Margaret's father Henry on 16 December 1907 at the Girvan Registry Office. As Bertie recalled, his mother regularly went out in the 1920s in all weathers with her father's horse and cart selling fish, fruit and other produce around the coastal town of Girvan. However, after meeting Joe Auld around 1930 she moved with him to Glasgow, getting a job in an east end bakery, and in 1931 Margaret and Joe were married.

John Lambie Auld, 27, an electrician's labourer, married wife Margaret Diamond Devlin, 25, a bakery worker, both residing at 752 London Road, Bridgeton, Glasgow on 16 October 1931 at Guthrie Memorial Church according to the forms of the Congregational Church. The wedding was conducted by Rev A B Halliday; the best man was John Lockhart, of 836 Shettleston Road, Glasgow and the best maid was Anna Devlin, Margaret's sister, of 426 London Road, Bridgeton. Coincidentally, when Joe and Margaret got married their home, at 752 London Road, Glasgow, was less than a mile from Celtic Park.

In 1934, Joe and Margaret moved to a small flat in Abercromby Street in the tough Calton district in Glasgow's east end, before being decanted across to the west end to live in Maryhill, where they raised their large family. Son Bertie was born in 1938 in a two-bedroomed council house at 95 Panmure Street, Maryhill, which even boasted an inside toilet. Back in those days most tenement flats in Glasgow still had shared toilets on the landings, so to have an inside toilet back then was seen as the height of luxury. Son Robert Auld was born on 23 March 1938 at 95 Panmure Street, Maryhill. The birth was registered by Bertie's father John, aka Joe, a builder's labourer, on 28 March 1938 at the Glasgow Registry Office.

Joe Auld was a crane-driver during the war and he was never out of work. Bertie's mother Margaret worked as a hawker, selling wares around the doors, becoming a 'weel-kent' face in Maryhill. As Bertie grew up his father Joe had a variety of jobs; as a pipe-layer, a brickie's labourer and also as a foundry labourer at the iron works between Firhill, Partick Thistle's ground, and Panmure Street. This was almost certainly the long-standing firm of Shaw & MacInnes Ltd who owned the Firhill Ironworks. Although Joe Auld was only 5ft 6in tall, he was a tough, wiry character and Bertie fondly remembered one job where his father traipsed around the streets with heavy metal buckets full of warm liquid tar maintaining potholes. Joe Auld was an extremely proud man when Bertie signed for Celtic in 1955.

Bertie's paternal grandparents – Robert Auld and Elizabeth Stewart

Bertie's grandfather Robert Auld was born around 1877 in Bridgeton, Glasgow to father Allan Auld, a confectioner, and mother Marion Montgomery. After leaving school Robert got a job in a weaving mill as a cotton factory labourer. His grandmother Elizabeth Stewart was born around 1878 to father Archibald Stewart, a master bootmaker, and mother Elizabeth Rogers. After schooling Elizabeth worked as a wincey weaver in a cotton mill factory, wincey being a type of warm fleecy cotton material. Those readers old enough may remember wearing their warm fleecy winceyette pyjamas in the winter time.

Robert Auld, 19, a cotton factory labourer, residing at 69 Downes Street, Bridgeton, Glasgow married wife Elizabeth Stewart, 18, a wincey weaver, residing at 24 Harvie Street, Bridgeton on 27 March 1896 at Elizabeth's home according to the forms of the Church of Scotland. The wedding was conducted by Rev John Hannay, minister in Calton; the best man was Martin Ward and the best maid was Matilda Boyd. Their son John Lambie Auld, aka Joe, was born on 27 August 1904 at 69 Harvie Street, Bridgeton, Glasgow. The birth was registered by Joe's mother Elizabeth on 13 September 1904 at the Glasgow Registry Office.

Robert Auld worked for many years in a balata belt making factory. Balata belts were manufactured using high quality cotton impregnated with balata gum and used particularly in conveyor belts for agricultural and industrial machinery. Robert was a widower by 1931, and his wife Elizabeth was dead by the time their son Joe was married.

Bertie's maternal grandparents – Henry Devlin and Wilhelmina McCrae

On Bertie's mother's side, his grandfather Henry Devlin, aka Harry, was born around 1880 in Girvan, Ayrshire to father John Devlin, a fish merchant, and mother Margaret Diamond. In 1891 census Henry, 11, resided at the unusually named Wreck Road, Girvan, which still exists today, with his parents and other siblings. When Harry left school he followed his father's trade and became a fish merchant too. His grandmother Wilhelmina McCrae was also born around 1881 to father James McCrae, a stone mason, and mother Annie Laurie.

In 1907 Harry and Wilhelmina were both residing at 27 Glendowne Street, Girvan, Ayrshire, when, for some reason, they travelled up to Glasgow to be married in a civil ceremony. That reason was obviously because Wilhelmina was seven months pregnant with their daughter Margaret and that Harry and Wilhelmina needed to get married, known in Glasgow as a 'huftie case'. Henry Devlin, 26, a fish merchant, married wife Wilhelmina McCrae, 26, both residing at 27 Glendowne Street, Girvan, on 18 September 1907 at 1 Duke Street, Dennistoun, Glasgow, by warrant of the Sheriff Substitute of Lanarkshire. The witnesses at the wedding were Bernard Blest, a butcher, and William Semple, a farm servant.

The fact that they had travelled up to Glasgow to marry in a civil ceremony, which was extremely rare in the late Victorian era, and not marry in a church in Girvan where they lived, suggests that Harry and Wilhelmina may have eloped. It is possible that they did not have the blessing of the local church or even their parents in order to get married. Their daughter Margaret Diamond Devlin was born six weeks later on St Andrew's Day, 30 November 1907, at 27 Glendowne Street, Girvan, Ayrshire. The birth was registered by Margaret's father Henry, a fish dealer, on 16 December 1907 at the Girvan Registry Office.

Bertie's great-grandparents

Bertie's great-grandparents were all born around the mid-19th century. On Bertie's paternal line his great-grandfather Allan Auld, who worked as a power loom weaver and then later as a confectioner, was born around 1839 and his great-grandmother Marion Montgomery was born around 1840, both in Kilmarnock, Ayrshire. Allan and Marion had two known sons born in Glasgow; Allan (b. ~1870) and Robert (b. ~1877) who was Bertie's grandfather. In 1881 census Allan Auld, 42, a power loom bustle tenter, resided at 266 London Road, Barrowfield, Glasgow with wife Marion, 41, sons Allan, 11, a scholar, and Robert, 3.

A tenter in a weaving factory was an early type of mechanic who would attend to the efficient working of the power looms. Allan at that time worked in a factory making bustles, a now obsolete expanded framework and that part of the drapery at the back of a Victorian woman's dress, which in those days was the absolute height of fashion. Allan Auld was dead before 1896, however, Marion Auld, nee Montgomery, Allan's widow, was still alive at that time.

Still on Bertie's paternal line his other great-grandfather was Archibald Stewart, a master bootmaker, and his great-grandmother was Elizabeth Rogers, although her surname has not been fully confirmed. They had a daughter Elizabeth (b. ~1878). Archibald and Elizabeth were both still alive in 1896.

On the maternal line Bertie's great-grandfather John Devlin, a fish merchant, was born around 1847 in Girvan, Ayrshire. His great-grandmother Margaret Diamond was also born there four years later around 1851. Girvan was a small bustling fishing port at that time facing the Ulster coast about fifty odd miles across the Irish Sea. John would go down to the harbour and fill up his cart each workday and hawk his fish around Girvan and the surrounding towns and villages. John and Margaret had six known children in Girvan, including son Henry (b. ~1880). In 1891 census John Devlin, 44, a fish hawker, resided at Wreck Road, Girvan with wife Margaret, 40, children Thomas, 15, also a fish hawker, then Hugh, 13, Henry, 11, Helen, 7, all at school, James, 3, and baby Margaret, 1. John and Margaret were both still alive in 1907.

Still on the maternal line his other great-grandfather was James McCrae, a stone mason, and his great-grandmother was Annie Laurie. They had a daughter Wilhelmina (b. ~1881). James McCrae was still alive in 1907 but his wife Annie McCrae, nee Laurie, was dead by that time.

There is a favourite old 17th century Scottish ballad penned by Captain William Douglas about a lost love sometimes called 'Bonnie Annie Laurie' although its proper title is 'Maxwelton Braes'. In the later Lady John Scott version published by James Lindsay in Glasgow, the song begins:-

Maxwelton Braes are bonnie,
Where early fa's the dew,
Twas there that Annie Laurie,
Gied me her promise true.

The song was effectively saved for the nation by Robert Burns in his collection of Scottish ballads. It was made famous by the great Scottish music-hall artist Sir Harry Lauder and also later recorded by the famous Irish tenor John McCormack. It would have been well known in the McCrae and Laurie household at that time and would likely have been a favoured song at family gatherings.

Chapter 11

Bobby Lennox (outside left)

Honours as a Celtic player:
1 European Cup
11 Scottish League titles
8 Scottish Cups
5 Scottish League Cups

The young Bobby Lennox

Bobby Lennox was born in Saltcoats, Ayrshire, for which he was jokingly dubbed to be the "outsider" in the Lisbon Lions team, having been born and raised the furthest distance away from the club than any of the others. Bobby Lennox is responsible for that renowned legend of the 30 mile radius of Parkhead, the others all being born within a 12 mile radius. The '30 miles' became a celebrated point which Lennox used to entitle his autobiography 'Thirty Miles to Paradise'. Robert Lennox, aka Bobby, was born on 30 August 1943, again during WWII, at 2 Quay Street, Saltcoats to father Robert Lennox, a shipyard labourer, and mother Agnes Erskine. The birth was registered by father Robert on 1 September 1943 at the Saltcoats Registry Office.

Bobby recorded his earliest memory of the club was when his father Robert took him as a boy to go and see Celtic play the Arsenal in the Coronation Cup in 1953. Bobby's recollection was that Bobby Collins scored from a corner kick and Celtic beat the Gunners 1-0. When he was younger his parents allowed him to go to watch local Ayrshire side Kilmarnock with his pals, but he was forbidden to go into Glasgow on his own. Eventually Bobby was allowed to go to Celtic Park with two of his friends to see a game against Airdrie and he remembered that Bertie Peacock scored the winning goal. It was quite a trek up from Saltcoats to Glasgow in those days. Bobby and his pals had to get the steam train into Glasgow and then get the Auchenshuggle tram up to Celtic Park.

Bobby signed provisional forms for the Hoops in September 1961 and in his early appearances he was an inauspicious striker and under Jimmy McGrory's regime Bobby's Celtic career was stumbling badly. He was even on the verge of a transfer to Falkirk FC for a modest fee to try and reboot his career. Matters thankfully changed in 1965 with the arrival of Jock Stein. Stein soon restructured the club and instilled into the team his modern footballing vision. Bobby was truly in Paradise and his career was now in the ascendancy.

Bobby's parents – Robert Lennox and Agnes Murphit Murray Dillon Erskine

Robert Lennox was born on 7 July 1899 at 6 Kirkgate Street, Saltcoats to father Andrew Lennox, a foundry labourer, and mother Susan Harris. The birth was registered by Robert's mother Susan on 22 July 1899 at the Saltcoats Registry Office.

After leaving school Robert became a shipyard labourer to trade. Bobby's mother Agnes Murphit Murray Dillon Erskine was born on 23 March 1906 at 5 Quay Street, Saltcoats to father Patrick Erskine, a hairdresser, and mother Isabella Dillon. The birth was registered by Agnes's father Patrick on 26 March 1906 at the Saltcoats Registry Office. It is possible that the forename registered as Murphit in Agnes's lengthy name may be a corruption of Murphy.

Robert Lennox, 29, a general labourer, residing at 39 Hamilton Street, Saltcoats married wife Agnes Murphit Murray Dillon Erskine, 22, a shop assistant, residing at 2 Quay Street, Saltcoats on Boxing Day, 26 December 1928, at St Mary's Chapel, Saltcoats according to the forms of the Roman Catholic Church. The wedding was conducted by Father John Rooney, assistant priest for Ardrossan district; the best man was Andrew Nicol, of 41 Springvale Street, Saltcoats and the best maid was Annie Erskine, Agnes's sister, of 2 Quay Street, Saltcoats.

By the outbreak of WWII Robert and Agnes were living at 2 Quay Street, Saltcoats and Robert was now a shipyard labourer, almost certainly employed in war service at nearby Ardrossan Harbour, renamed by the Admiralty as HMS Fortitude. The huge Royal Navy Fleet was anchored just offshore from Saltcoats in the Clyde estuary and there would have been plenty of maintenance work for Robert's shipyard. On 27 March 1943, the American-built lend-lease carrier HMS Dasher sank just between Ardrossan and Brodick, following an accidental explosion during aeroplane refuelling, with the loss of 379 lives.

Five months later, Robert Lennox, aka Bobby, was born on 30 August 1943 at 2 Quay Street, Saltcoats. The birth was registered by father Robert, a shipyard labourer, on 1 September 1943 at the Saltcoats Registry Office. Bobby's father Robert was a huge Celtic fan and on 11 May 1953 he took his son to see Celtic beat the Arsenal 1-0 in front of a 60,000 crowd at Parkhead in the Coronation Cup, held to celebrate Queen Elizabeth II's accession to the throne.

Incidentally, Celtic beat Hibs 2-0 in the final at Hampden Park in front of an incredible crowd of 117,000. Among that great side, managed by Jimmy McGrory, were Celtic legends including Bobby Evans, Charlie Tully and Bobby Collins and significantly, two of the Lisbon Lions' management team – Jock Stein and Neil Mochan. As young Bobby got older Robert allowed him to take the steam train up to Glasgow with his pals to follow his beloved Celtic, 30 miles away in Paradise.

Bobby's paternal grandparents – Andrew Lennox and Susan Harris

Bobby's grandfather Andrew Lennox was born around 1870 to father Patrick Lennox, a stone mason, and mother Margaret Duggan. After leaving school Andrew worked as a quay labourer at Ardrossan Harbour. Bobby's grandmother Susan Harris was born around 1873 to father Robert Harris, an aerated water manufacturer, and mother Susan Guthrie. After schooling and certainly by 1892 Susan was employed as a dynamite factory worker at the Nobel Works at Ardeer, between Stevenston and Irvine, on the Ayrshire coast. The Ardeer factory was one of many owned and built by Alfred Nobel, the Swedish scientist, famed for the Nobel Peace Prize. This was dangerous work but many young girls were employed because of their nimble fingers in handling high explosives.

The Glasgow Herald reported explosions at Ardeer on 8 May 1884, when a number of girls were instantaneously killed, on 18 April 1887 on a Saturday morning with no fatalities, and again on 29 January 1901, when one girl was killed, when frozen unworkable dynamite was being moved in error from one hut to another.

The author's great-great-grandfather George Caie Clark, Annie Collie's grandfather, was transferred on 29 April 1916 from the Scottish Rifles (Cameronians) during WWI to serve with 206 'P' Company Royal Defence Corps to protect the Ardeer Nobel Works from German saboteurs. The army had discovered that volunteer George was actually 58 years old. Instead of demobbing him, he was assigned to the RDC, which was effectively the home guard regiment during WWI.

Andrew Lennox, 22, a quay labourer, residing at 5 Harbour Lane, Ardrossan married wife Susan Harris, 19, a dynamite factory worker, residing at Quay Street, Saltcoats on 6 September 1892 at the Roman Catholic Chapel, Saltcoats, according to the forms of the Roman Catholic Church. The wedding was conducted by Father James MacKintosh, RC clergyman; the best man was Arthur McQuade and the best maid was Agnes Murphy. Andrew, by then a foundry labourer, and Susan's son Robert was born on 7 July 1899 at 6 Kirkgate Street, Saltcoats, Ayrshire. The birth was registered by Robert's mother Susan on 22 July 1899 at the Saltcoats Registry Office. Andrew and Susan were both still alive in 1928 when their son Robert was married.

Bobby's maternal grandparents – Patrick Erskine and Isabella Dillon

On Bobby's maternal side his grandfather Patrick Erskine was born around 1886 to father Patrick Erskine, a dock labourer, and mother Annie McAvoy. When Patrick left school he apprenticed to become a hairdresser in Ardrossan. Bobby's grandmother Isabella Dillon was also born around that same year in 1886 to father James Dillon, a general dealer, and mother Agnes Murray. Isabella grew up in Saltcoats where Bobby was later to be born. It was mentioned in the preface that the author was taken to Celtic Park for the first time in 1970 by an upstairs neighbour in Pollok named John Dillon.

Patrick Erskine, 19, a hairdresser, residing at 33 Glasgow Street, Ardrossan married wife Isabella Dillon, also 19, residing at 17 Quay Street, Saltcoats on 2 October 1905 at the Roman Catholic Chapel, Saltcoats, according to the forms of the Roman Catholic Church. The wedding was conducted by Father William Keogh; the best man was Hugh Lynch and the best maid was Jeanie Dillon, Isabella's sister. Patrick and Isabella had two known daughters; Agnes and Annie. Their daughter Agnes Murphit Murray Dillon Erskine was born on 23 March 1906 at 5 Quay Street, Saltcoats. The birth was registered by Agnes's father Patrick on 26 March 1906 at the Saltcoats Registry Office. Patrick, a hairdresser, and Isabella were both still alive in 1928 when their daughter Agnes married Robert Lennox.

Bobby's great-grandparents

Bobby's great-grandparents were all born around the mid-19th century. On Bobby's paternal line his great-grandfather was Patrick Lennox, a stone mason, and his great-grandmother was Margaret Duggan and they had a son Andrew (b. ~1870). Patrick and Margaret were both deceased by 1892. Still on Bobby's paternal line his other great-grandfather was Robert Harris, an aerated water manufacturer running his own business, and his great-grandmother was Susan Guthrie and they had a daughter Susan (b. ~1873). Robert and Susan were still alive in 1892 and living in Quay Street, Saltcoats.

On the maternal line Bobby's great-grandfather was Patrick Erskine, a dock labourer at Ardrossan Harbour, and his great-grandmother was Annie McAvoy. Patrick and Annie had a son Patrick (b. ~1886). In 1905, Patrick Erskine was a widower living at Glasgow Street, Ardrossan and his wife Annie was dead by then. Still on the maternal line his other great-grandfather was James Dillon, a general dealer, and his great-grandmother was Agnes Murray and they had two known daughters; Isabella (b. ~1886) and Jeanie. A near neighbour of Robert Harris, James Dillon was also a widower in 1905 living in Quay Street, Saltcoats, and his wife Agnes was dead by that time.

Part 2:

The other Lisbon Lions players
1966 – 1967

Campaign medallists

Chapter 12

John Fallon (goalkeeper)

Honours as a Celtic player:

1 European Cup

7 Scottish League titles

2 Scottish Cups

3 Scottish League Cups

The young John Fallon

Against the backdrop of the Battle of Britain, which was being waged in the skies by the RAF against the German Luftwaffe, John James Fallon was born on 16 August 1940 at 13 Letterickhills Crescent, Cambuslang, Lanarkshire to father Patrick Fallon, a colliery underground fireman, and mother Jane Murray. The birth was registered by John's father Patrick on 19 August 1940 at the Cambuslang Registry Office. Born into a big Celtic-supporting family in Cambuslang, John was a member of the James Kelly Celtic Supporters Club in Blantyre from an early age. He paid a mere seven pence to get into Celtic Park as a boy and fondly recalled in his autobiography, 'Keeping in Paradise', overnight trips as a supporter to far-flung Aberdeen in the early 1950s, as well as the shorter runs to Dundee and Edinburgh. He watched on as Celtic lifted the Coronation Cup in 1953, followed by the league and cup double under captain Jock Stein in 1953-54 and also when Celtic beat Rangers in the record-breaking 7-1 League Cup final of 1957.

John was signed on as a young junior from Fauldhouse United by Celtic on 11 December 1958 and he was soon promoted to cover for the famous eccentric keeper Frank Haffey. In 1961 Haffey took the blame for the 9-3 defeat Scotland suffered against the 'Auld Enemy' England and he never played for Scotland again. The ex-Celt (1947-49) and legendary manager Tommy Docherty often related to guests in after-dinner speeches that the blame for the loss lay squarely on the fact the ball was coloured orange. Docherty joked that in that losing Scotland team the Celtic players refused to touch the ball and the Rangers players refused to kick the ball.

John Fallon played his first full game for the Celtic first team on 26 September 1959 in a 1-1 draw against the 'Bully Wee' Clyde and he replaced Haffey completely in 1963. However, in spite of a successful European campaign in 1964 when Celtic reached the semi-finals, John lost his place as first choice keeper to the more experienced Ronnie Simpson after Jock Stein arrived as manager in 1965. Fallon good-naturedly understudied Simpson for the next couple of years, with Stein playing him only occasionally against 'easy opponents'. When John was later interviewed, he said it was more nerve-racking sitting on the bench as substitute than it was being on the field. In his autobiography, John described a fractious relationship with Jock Stein. He felt it was through Stein he missed out on the chance to play for Scotland and also for Ireland, which he qualified to play for through his grandfather Patrick Fallon.

Fallon played in goal for Celtic between December 1958 and February 1972 and he remains a proud member of the famous Lisbon Lions team of 1967. In some ways Fallon will be remembered as the only medal winning player who never actually played a game in the 1966–67 European Cup campaign. John received his medal in recognition for being the substitute goalkeeper in Lisbon, goalies being the only substitutes allowed in those days. But the bottom line is no-one can take away the fact that John Fallon earned the right to hold one of those distinguished medals, proclaiming him as a true Lion.

John's parents – Patrick Fallon and Jane Murray

Patrick Fallon was born on 8 June 1902 at 25 Old Row, Newton, Cambuslang to father Patrick Fallon, a coal miner, and mother Catherine Murphy. The birth was registered by Patrick's father Patrick on 13 June 1902 at the Cambuslang Registry Office. In 1911 census Patrick, 8, at school, resided at 39 Caldervale Terrace, Stonefield, Blantyre with his parents and siblings. After leaving school Patrick became a coal miner at Blantyre Ferme Colliery, Lanarkshire, like his father before him.

Patrick would find coal mining to be a brutally hard and dangerous occupation at Blantyre Ferme Colliery. For instance, on Monday morning of 18 July 1921 a serious explosion, resulting in the death of four men and injuries to two others, occurred in Blantyre Ferme Colliery, near

Uddingston. The colliery at that time belonged to Messrs. A. G. Moore and Company Limited. It is unknown whether Patrick, who would have been 19 at the time, worked on that fatal shift, but fortunately he was not one of the dead or injured on that terrible morning.

John's mother Jane Murray was born on 15 April 1907 at 74 Westburn Rows, Cambuslang to father William Murray, a coal miner, and mother Helen Sherry. The birth was registered by Jane's father William Murray on 20 April 1907 at the Cambuslang Registry Office. After leaving school Jane went to work as a weaver in a cotton factory. Patrick Fallon, 26, a coal miner, residing at Blantyre Ferme, Uddingston married wife Jane Murray, 21, a cotton factory weaver, residing at 27 Montgomery Place, Newton, Cambuslang on Christmas Day, 25 December 1928, at St Charles Chapel, Newton, Cambuslang according to the forms of the Roman Catholic Church. The wedding was conducted by Father George Galbraith, priest at St Charles Chapel, Hallside, Newton; the best man was Thomas Fallon, Patrick's brother, of Blantyre Ferme and the best maid was Sarah Murray, Jane's sister, of 27 Montgomery Place, Newton.

By the outbreak of WWII Patrick, then working as an underground colliery fireman, and Jane were living at Letterickhills Crescent, Cambuslang. Son John James Fallon was born on 16 August 1940 at 13 Letterickhills Crescent, Cambuslang. The birth was registered by John's father Patrick on 19 August 1940 at the Cambuslang Registry Office.

John's paternal grandparents – Patrick Fallon and Catherine Murphy

John's grandfather Patrick Fallon was born around 1876 in Ireland to father Patrick Fallon, a farmer in County Sligo, Ireland, and mother Mary Lang. John Fallon remains immensely proud of his Sligo roots. After leaving school Patrick worked as a miner in the Lanarkshire coalfields. John's grandmother Catherine Murphy was born around 1883 in Tollcross, Glasgow to father John Murphy, a colliery labourer, and mother Elizabeth Cassidy. After schooling, and like many young girls of the Victorian era, Catherine was employed as a domestic servant. The observant reader will have noticed Stevie Chalmer's great-grandmother was also named Catherine Murphy, although, in fairness, Catherine Murphy is a common Irish name and there is no suggestion of any direct relationship.

Patrick Fallon, 26, a coal miner, married wife Catherine Murphy, 19, a domestic servant, both residing at 25 Old Rows, Newton, Cambuslang on New Year's Day, 1 January 1902, at St Charles Chapel, Newton, Cambuslang according to the forms of the Roman Catholic Church. The wedding was conducted by Father Louis de Mentinsere; the best man was Bernard Devine and the best maid was Maggie Loughrie.

Patrick and Catherine had four known children in Lanarkshire; Patrick (b. 1902, Cambuslang), Lizzie (b. ~1904, Uddingston), Thomas (b. ~1908, Uddingston) and Margaret (b. ~1910, Uddingston). Their son Patrick Fallon was born on 8 June 1902 at 25 Old Row, Newton, Cambuslang. The birth was registered by Patrick's father Patrick on 13 June 1902 at the Cambuslang Registry Office.

In 1911 census Patrick Fallon, 36, a coal miner hewer at a colliery, resided at 39 Caldervale Terrace, Stonefield, Blantyre with wife Catherine, 28, children Patrick, 8, at school, Lizzie, 7, at school, Thomas, 3, and baby Margaret, 1. The census showed they had been married for nine years with four children and none had died in infancy. Patrick, a widowed coal miner at Blantyre Ferme Colliery near Uddingston, which was owned by Messrs A. G. Moore & Coy. Ltd, was still alive in 1928 and his wife Catherine was dead by then.

John's maternal grandparents – William Murray and Helen Sherry

On John's maternal side his grandfather William Murray was born around 1883 to father Michael Murray, a pit sinker, and mother Agnes Sime. When William left school he also became a coal miner in Lanarkshire. John's grandmother Helen Sherry was born around 1885 to father Daniel Sherry, a coal miner, and mother Jane Kelly. Just like young Catherine Murphy, after leaving school, Helen became a domestic servant in Cambuslang.

William Murray, 23, a coal miner, residing at 54 Dunlop Street, Newton, Cambuslang married wife Helen Sherry, 21, residing at 6 Pitt Street, Newton, Cambuslang on 28 December 1906 at St Charles Chapel, Newton, Cambuslang, according to the forms of the Roman Catholic Church. The wedding was conducted by Father James Joseph Doyle; the best man was Edward Keenan and the best maid was Mary Callaghan. William and Helen had two known daughters;

Jane and Sarah. Their daughter Jane Murray was born on 15 April 1907 at 74 Westburn Rows, Cambuslang. The birth was registered by Jane's father William on 20 April 1907 at the Cambuslang Registry Office. William, a coal miner, and Helen were both still alive in 1928 when their daughter Jane married Patrick Fallon.

John's great-grandparents

John's great-grandparents were all born around the mid-19th century and most likely all in Ireland around about the time of the infamous Irish Potato Famine (1848-52). During this period it is estimated around one million Irish perished through disease, destitution and starvation and about another one million Irish emigrated to mainland Britain and further afield to USA, Canada, Australia and New Zealand.

On John's paternal line his great-grandfather was Patrick Fallon, a farmer in County Sligo, and his great-grandmother was Mary Lang and they had a son Patrick (b. ~1876, County Sligo). Patrick Fallon was recorded as a farmer in Ireland, which generally meant a subsistence smallholding crofter. Patrick and Mary were still alive in 1902 when their son Patrick married in Cambuslang, Lanarkshire.

Still on John's paternal line his other great-grandfather was John Murphy, a colliery labourer, and his great-grandmother was Elizabeth Cassidy and they had a daughter Catherine (b. ~1883, Tollcross, Glasgow). It is likely that John Murphy worked at Bogleshole Colliery in Tollcross, owned by James Dunlop & Coy. Ltd who also ran the renowned Clyde Ironworks. John and Elizabeth were still alive in 1902 when their daughter Catherine married in Cambuslang.

On the maternal line John's great-grandfather was Michael Murray, a pit sinker, and his great-grandmother was Agnes Sime. A pit sinker was employed to sink the shafts down to the coal seams and at that time new shafts were being sunk on a regular basis. Michael and Agnes had a son William (b. ~1883). Michael, a pit sinker, and Agnes were both still alive in 1906 when son William married in Cambuslang. Still on the maternal line his other great-grandfather was Daniel Sherry, a coal miner, and his great-grandmother was Jane Kelly and they had a daughter Helen (b. ~1885). Daniel Sherry was a widower in 1906 living in Newton, Cambuslang. His wife Jane was dead by that time.

Chapter 13

Joe McBride (centre forward)

Honours as a Celtic player:
1 European Cup
2 Scottish League titles
2 Scottish League Cups

The young Joe McBride

Joe McBride played for various clubs including Celtic, Hibernian, Motherwell and Dunfermline Athletic. He was a prolific striker and he gained the third highest tally of goals in the Scottish League since football resumed after the end of WWII. He also represented both Scotland and the Scottish League at international level. Joe was born in Govan, just a stone's throw from the home of Glasgow Rangers, although that was not the team that Joe ever had aspirations to play for. Joseph McBride was born on 10 June 1938 at 16 Napier Street, Tradeston, Govan to father James McBride, a shipwright journeyman, and mother Beatrice McGowan. The birth was registered by Joe's father James on 20 June 1938 at the Glasgow Registry Office.

Joe attended St. Gerard's RC Secondary School, Govan and he was a prolific goal scorer for the school's teams. He signed for Kilmarnock when he was 15 and was loaned out to junior side Kirkintilloch Rob Roy. He made an immediate impact at Rob Roy and he was quickly brought back into the Kilmarnock first team. Joe was sold to Wolverhampton Wanderers in 1959 for £12,500, a significant transfer fee at the time. However, he failed to settle in England and did not even make a first team appearance for Wolves. After short spells with Luton Town and then back up to Partick Thistle, his career took off when he signed for Motherwell in 1962. Joe was Motherwell's top goal scorer in three successive seasons, which attracted the attention of newly appointed Celtic manager Jock Stein, who signed him on at Parkhead for a fee of £22,000 in 1965.

Alongside a young Alex Ferguson, at that time playing for Dunfermline Athletic, Joe was the top goal scorer in the 1965–66 season with 31 goals. He again was scoring prolifically during the legendary 1966–67 season, but Joe suffered a serious injury in December 1966. This injury meant, although Joe was part of the Lisbon Lions' squad, he did not play in the 1967 European Cup Final. Instead, Stein picked Stevie Chalmers for the centre-forward position in Lisbon and, as fate would have it, Chalmers scored the triumphant goal.

However, without Joe McBride's significant contribution in the pre-Christmas campaign, prior to his injury, Celtic may not have marched on to Lisbon and the award of his European Cup medal is wholly justified. Jock Stein was a great admirer of his striking prowess but the last word on Joe must go to that other Celtic legend, Jimmy McGrory, who stated, "Joe McBride was the finest Celtic centre-forward that I have ever seen playing".

Joe's parents – James McBride and Beatrice McGowan

James McBride was born on 25 August 1904 at 467 Govan Road, Govan, Glasgow to father Alexander McBride, a spirit salesman, and mother Catherine O'Neill. The birth was registered by James's father Alexander on 7 September 1904 at the Govan Registry Office. After leaving school James went to work in the world-famous Govan shipyards. Shipbuilding on the Clyde at that time was at its zenith, churning out some of the biggest and best vessels for the British and world markets on an unprecedented scale. Production peaked up to and during WWI, when the Royal Navy was demanding Dreadnought battlecruisers, frigates and other warships to rival the fearsome German Imperial Battle fleet.

The Govan yards were later hit badly during the Great Depression of the 1920s and 30s, with production levels rising again during WWII. However, into the 1950s and 60s Clyde shipbuilding went into a gradual decline due to worldwide competition and it reached its low point in the 1980s during Margaret Thatcher's 'industrial and manufacturing restructuring'. The yards at Govan and Scotstoun now specialise in the construction of modern kit-built Royal Naval vessels.

Joe's mother Beatrice was born as Bridget McGowan on 18 March 1907 at 7 Albert Street, Govan to father Michael McGowan, also a shipyard labourer, and mother Bridget McGowan. The birth was registered by Beatrice's mother Bridget on 8 April 1907 at the Govan Registry Office. After leaving school Beatrice went to work as a tea room waitress.

Nowadays, towns and cities are proliferated by a plethora of coffee shops but in the Edwardian era the Glasgow tea room reigned supreme. Tea rooms like Lipton's, Lyons and the Ca D'oro Building, designed by John Honeyman were dotted around the city, but the most famous was Miss Cranston's Willow Tea Rooms, designed by the famous Glasgow architect Charles Rennie Mackintosh, another Allan Glen's boy. Interestingly, Mackintosh, who was born just around the corner from St Mungo's Retreat in Townhead, also became a partner with John Honeyman at Honeyman, Keppie and Mackintosh (Architects).

James McBride, 22, an apprentice shipwright, residing at 3 Shandon Street, Govan married wife Beatrice McGowan, 19, a tea room waitress, residing at 19 Albert Street, Govan on 29 October 1926 at St Saviour's Chapel, Govan according to the forms of the Roman Catholic Church. The wedding was conducted by Father Thomas Doyle, RC clergyman at St Saviour's Chapel; the best man was William Harle, of 586 Govan Road, and the best maid was Jean McGowan, Beatrice's sister, also of 19 Albert Street. Their son Joseph McBride, aka Joe, was born on 10 June 1938 at 16 Napier Street, Tradeston. The birth was registered by father James on 20 June 1938 at the Glasgow Registry Office.

Joe's paternal grandparents – Alexander McBride and Catherine O'Neill

Joe's grandfather Alexander McBride was born around 1861 to father Neil McBride, a carter, and mother Mary Neil. After leaving school it appears that Alexander apprenticed to work as a saddler, however, by the time he married in 1893 he was working as a spirit salesman. Alexander would have had little trouble selling his spirit wares, because the parish of Govan had one of the highest densities of public houses in Glasgow, to quench the thirst of the hard-grafting and drouthy shipbuilders. Joe's grandmother Catherine O'Neill was born around 1866 to father Joseph O'Neill, a coal merchant, and mother Mary Harkins.

Alexander McBride, 32, a spirit salesman, residing at 62 Queen Street, Govan married wife Catherine O'Neill, 27, residing at 24 Paisley Road West, Kinning Park, Glasgow on 14 February 1893 at St Margaret's Church, Kinning Park according to the forms of the Roman Catholic Church. The wedding was conducted by Father John J Sheehy; the best man was Robert Watt and the best maid was Martha O'Neill, Catherine's sister. Alexander and Catherine had a son James (b. 1904, Govan). Their son James McBride was born on 25 August 1904 at 467 Govan Road, Govan, Glasgow. The birth was registered by James's father Alexander, a spirit salesman, on 7 September 1904 at the Govan Registry Office. Alexander, recorded as a saddler, was dead by 1926 and his wife Catherine was a widow at that time.

Joe's maternal grandparents – Michael McGowan and Bridget McGowan

On Joe's maternal side his grandfather Michael McGowan was born around 1871 to father Michael McGowan, an Irish farm labourer, and mother Catherine McCormick. When Michael left school he became an apprentice in the Govan shipbuilding industry. Joe's grandmother Bridget McGowan was born around 1879 to another unrelated McGowan line, although her father was also coincidentally named Michael McGowan, another shipyard labourer, and her mother was Catherine Gallagher. When Bridget left school she got a job as a preserve work worker. Bridget most likely worked at John Gray & Sons Wholesale and Export Confectioners, who had a factory at 20 Commercial Road, Gorbals, Glasgow and were famed for their Scotch Marmalade.

Michael McGowan, 26, a shipyard labourer, residing at 22 Victoria Street, Govan married wife Bridget McGowan, 19, residing at 18 Victoria Street, Govan on Hogmanay, 31 December 1896, at St Anthony's Chapel, Govan according to the forms of the Roman Catholic Church. The wedding was conducted by Father G McBrearty, RC clergyman; the best man was William McGowan and the best maid was Maggie Feechan. It may also be noted that Father G McBrearty also conducted the wedding of Jim Craig's ancestors Patrick Hughes and Annie Bridget Wisdom in 1909 at St Anthony's Chapel in Govan. "We're a' Jock Tamson's bairns".

Michael and Bridget had two known daughters; Bridget and Jean. Their daughter Beatrice was born as Bridget McGowan on 18 March 1907 at 7 Albert Street, Govan. The birth was registered by Beatrice's mother Bridget on 8 April 1907 at the Govan Registry Office. Michael, a shipyard labourer, and Bridget were both still alive in 1926 when their daughter Beatrice married James McBride.

Joe's great-grandparents

Joe's great-grandparents were all born around the mid-19th century and most, if not all, in Ireland about the time of the infamous Irish Potato Famine (1848-52). On Joe's paternal line, his great-grandfather was Neil McBride, a carter, and his great-grandmother was Mary Neil and they had a son Alexander (b. ~1861). Neil was dead by 1893 and his wife Mary was a widow at that time. Still on Joe's paternal line, his other great-grandfather was Joseph O'Neill, a coal merchant, and his great-grandmother was Mary Harkins and they had two known daughters; Catherine (b. ~1866) and Martha. Joseph O'Neill was also dead by 1893 and his wife Mary was a widow at that time.

On the maternal line Joe's great-grandfather was Michael McGowan, a farm labourer, and his great-grandmother was Catherine McCormick. Michael and Catherine had a son Michael (b. ~1871). Michael was dead by 1897 as his wife Catherine was a widow by then. Still on the maternal line, his other great-grandfather was another unrelated Michael McGowan, a shipyard labourer, and his great-grandmother was Catherine Gallagher and they had a daughter Bridget (b. ~1879). Michael, a shipyard labourer, and his wife Catherine were both still alive in 1897 and probably living in Victoria Street, Govan.

Chapter 14

Charlie Gallagher (inside forward)

Honours as a Celtic player:

1 European Cup

3 Scottish League titles

1 Scottish Cup

1 Scottish League Cup

The young Charlie Gallagher

Charles James Gallagher, aka Charlie, was born on 3 November 1940 at the Southern General Hospital, Govan, Glasgow to father Daniel Gallagher, a builder's labourer, and mother Anne Duffy. The birth was registered by Charlie's father Daniel on 18 November 1940 at the Glasgow Registry Office. At that time the Gallagher family were living at 14 Salisbury Street, Gorbals, the district synonymous with Glasgow's violent, slum-ridden 'No Mean City' reputation. Charlie forged his way out of the tough Gorbals environment by using his gifted feet. The Gorbals Bhoy signed for his beloved Celtic, from Yoker Athletic, in September 1958. The inside-forward made his Hoops debut in a 1-0 League Cup victory at home to Raith Rovers in August 1959 and he went on to make 171 appearances and net 32 goals in a 12 year Parkhead career.

Charlie was an assured, if unspectacular player. He was also the cousin of Celtic and Manchester United legend - Paddy Crerand. Crerand went on to win the European Cup with the Reds the following year in 1968, alongside Bobby Charlton, George Best and Denis Law. Charlie and Paddy both attended Holyrood Secondary School on the south side of Glasgow. The author's mother Margaret McCue also attended Holyrood about four years before these Celtic greats. Charlie may have lacked pace and aggression but he was a wonderful passer of the ball and possessed a thunderous shot. He was always willing to work for his teammates and he was unlucky that during his time at Celtic he had to compete with the magnificent Bertie Auld for a starting position. Gallagher's first memorable game for the Parkhead club was the 3-1 win at home to Glasgow Rangers in September 1964 played in heavy underfoot conditions.

Charlie suffered from some inconsistency in his early years when Jimmy McGrory was manager. However, the arrival of Jock Stein as manager brought out the best in him and Stein always played him in a modern two-man midfield system. He had a fine game in the 1965 Scottish Cup final victory against Dunfermline when Billy McNeill scored the winner from a glorious corner from Gallagher. Ironically, he also took the corner from which big Cesar again scored the winner against the top Yugoslavian side Vojvodina in the European Cup quarter final tie of March 1967 and Charlie may have felt a little unlucky not to have played in Lisbon. However, for his valiant efforts during that historic campaign Stein made sure that UEFA issued Charlie with his winners' medal - another true Lisbon Lion.

Charlie's parents – Daniel Gallagher and Anne Duffy

Daniel Gallagher, aka Dan, was born on 29 January 1904, in Magheraclogher, Tullaghobegly, County Donegal on the Atlantic coast around thirty miles west of Letterkenny, to father Daniel Gallagher, a smallholding farmer, and mother Ellen Boyle. In 1911 census Dan, 7, a scholar, was living at house No.19, a small farm at Magheraclogher, County Donegal, with his parents and other siblings. Charlie's mother Anne Duffy was born on 30 July 1904 again most likely in County Donegal to father Charles Duffy, a labourer, and mother Rose Harkin.

That remote area around Magheraclogher and Buncrana in west Donegal was renowned as 'Bandit Country'. It was a hotbed of tough, uncompromising men, whose offspring became mobsters in New York City and Boston and with a strong Fenian support base, many Donegal men also joined the Irish Republican Army (IRA). After the uprisings in 1916 and 1918, the Irish War of Independence was fought between the IRA and the British Army from 1919 until 1921, culminating in the formation of the Irish Free State. From 1922 to 1937 Donegal was in that part of Ireland called the Irish Free State and in 1937 it became part of the Republic of Ireland.

Two years later, Daniel Gallagher, 35, a labourer, married wife Anne Duffy, 35, on 3 May 1939 in Letterkenny, County Donegal in St Eunan's Cathedral, according to the forms of the Roman Catholic Church. It appears that Daniel and Anne had returned to Letterkenny from Glasgow by crossing the Irish border via the port of Londonderry, in County Derry, in the newly formed Northern Ireland. Now more commonly named Derry City, Londonderry had regular steamer sailings for Glasgow and Clyde ports. On their marriage certificate both stated that they lived in St John's in the parish of the Gorbals at the time of the wedding and their witnesses were Michael Peoples and Rose Coll. Michael and Rose were most likely from Magheraclogher village too as these are both common surnames from there. It is likely that Rose Coll was closely related to Peter and Vincent 'Mad Dog' Coll who will be discussed later in the chapter.

Very soon after their wedding Daniel and Anne returned to live and work in the deprived Glaswegian slum district of the Gorbals. They were certainly in the Gorbals by the spring of 1940 as the Battle of Britain raged on above them. Anne fell pregnant with Charlie and Daniel got a job as a builder's labourer. Son Charles James Gallagher was born on 3 November 1940 at the Southern General Hospital, Govan. The birth was registered by Charlie's father Daniel on 18 November 1940 at the Glasgow Registry Office. At that time Daniel and Anne were living at 14 Salisbury Street, Gorbals.

In the 1950s, the Glasgow Corporation embarked on a huge programme of slum clearance and much of the old Gorbals was demolished. Many of the tenants, like Daniel and Anne, were moved to the new suburban housing estates. Daniel and Anne relocated to their new home at 16 Holmbyre Road, Castlemilk, situated in the south east suburbs of Glasgow. Castlemilk Estate lay in the ancient lands of Cassilton of Carmunnock and it was the summer residence of the Stewarts of Castlemilk, who owned their large farming estate of Castlemilk near Lockerbie in Dumfriesshire. In the 18th century the Stewarts, distant cousins of the Royal Stewart line, built their huge mansion near Glasgow, in order that they could conduct business in the city. They named it Castlemilk House. In the 1950s and 60s Castlemilk House became a children's home, but it was demolished in 1969, although the old stable block has now been renovated and converted to offices in 2006.

Charlie's mother Anne Gallagher nee Duffy, 74, died on 19 July 1979 at 16 Holmbyre Road, Castlemilk and Charlie, then living in Dumbarton, registered the death on the following day, 20 July 1979, at the Glasgow Registry Office. Charlie's father Daniel Gallagher, 87, a retired builder's labourer, still residing at 16 Holmbyre Road, Castlemilk, died on the morning of 9 December 1991 at the Victoria Infirmary, Battlefield. Charlie, by then residing in Bishopbriggs, registered the death later that day at the Glasgow Registry Office.

In another piece of coincidental Glaswegian history, the site of Battlefield in Langside is synonymous with another of the Royal Stewarts as it was the location of Mary Queen of Scots short, sharp defeat on 13 May 1568, effectively bringing her reign to an end.

Charlie's paternal grandparents – Daniel Gallagher and Ellen Boyle

Charlie's grandfather Daniel Gallagher was born around 1858 in Magheraclogher, County Donegal to father Henry Gallagher and mother Catherine McFadden. Charlie's grandmother Ellen Boyle was born on 12 October 1867 also in Magheraclogher, County Donegal to father Daniel Boyle and mother Sarah Doherty, aka Sally. Daniel Gallagher, a smallholding farmer, married wife Ellen Boyle on 13 February 1888 in the Magheraclogher Roman Catholic Church; the witnesses were Doalty Gallagher and Bridget McGarvey.

Daniel and Ellen had ten known children; Henry (b. ~1890), Sarah (b. ~1892), John, aka Shane (b. ~1894), Margaret (b. ~1896), Bridget, aka Biddy (b. ~1899), Catherine, aka Kate (b. ~1901), Daniel, aka Dan (b. 29 January 1904), Charles (b. ~1906), Patrick (b. ~1908) and Mary (b. ~1913). Son Daniel Gallagher was born on 29 January 1904 in Magheraclogher, County Donegal.

In 1901 census of Ireland the family resided at household No.56, a smallholding farm in Magheraclogher, Tullaghobegly, County Donegal. Daniel Gallagher, 43, a farmer, resided there with wife Ellen, 30, a farmer's wife, children Henry, 11, a scholar, Sarah, 8, a scholar, Shane, 7, a scholar, Maggie, 4, a scholar, Biddey, 2. Also residing there was Daniel's widowed mother Catherine, 60, and his unmarried sister Maggie, 28, a domestic servant.

Also in the village at household No.18 resided Toal Coll, a farmer, and his wife Annie Duncan. They went on to have six children and in 1907 and 1908 respectively, they bore two sons Peter and Vincent Coll. Peter and Vincent emigrated to the notorious Bronx district in New York and became mobsters in New York City, originally as beer truck guards for Dutch Schultz. Vincent Coll married the infamous gangster's moll Lottie Kreisberger. In 1931 Vincent 'Mad Dog' Coll and his brother Peter started an ugly turf war against Schultz and Owney Madden. They were also implicated in ransom-based kidnappings including Rudi Vallee, Sherman Billingsly and George 'Big Frenchy' de Mange. Early in 1931 Peter Coll was machine gunned down in a Harlem street and his brother Vincent went on the lam. 'Mad Dog' returned to New York and threatened to kidnap his one-time mobster accomplice, Owney Madden, Madden and Dutch Schultz decided there was only one way to resolve the issue. Just after midnight on 8 February 1932, 'Mad Dog' Coll died in a hail of machine gun bullets in a phone booth as he argued vociferously with Madden from within the New London Pharmacy and Candy Shop.

In 1911 census of Ireland the Gallagher family resided at household No.19, their smallholding farm in Magheraclogher, County Donegal, which was the same house where the family had lived since 1901. Daniel Gallagher, 53, a Roman Catholic farmer, resided there with wife Ellen, 41, children Henry, 21, a labourer, Sarah, 19, Shane, 17, a school monitor, Biddy, 12, at school, Dan, 7, also at school, and Charles, 5. The record also shows Daniel's elderly widowed mother Catherine Gallagher, 76 (b. ~1835, Co. Donegal), as head of household, and his sister Maggie, 40 (b. ~1871, Co. Donegal), residing at the Magheraclogher farm.

The census also records that Daniel and Ellen had been married for twenty three years and in total they bore ten children, with only six still alive by 1911. Dan and Ellen had fallen victim to the scourge of the high infant mortality rates suffered in the Victorian and Edwardian eras. Daniel, a farmer, and Ellen were both dead by 1991 as recorded by Charlie Gallagher on his father Daniel's death certificate, although they would both be long dead before that date.

144

Charlie's maternal grandparents – Charles Duffy and Rose Harkin

On Charlie's maternal side his grandfather Charles Duffy, whom Charlie was named after, and his grandmother Rose Harkin were born around the 1870s most likely in County Donegal, Ireland. Charles Duffy, a labourer, married wife Rose Harkin and they had a daughter Anne (b. 30 July 1904). Charles Duffy, a labourer, and Rose were both dead by 1979 as recorded by Charlie Gallagher on his mother Anne's death certificate.

Charlie's great-grandparents

On Charlie's paternal side his great-grandfather was Henry Gallagher and his great-grandmother was Catherine McFadden both born around 1835 and most likely in Magheraclogher, County Donegal. Henry Gallagher married wife Catherine McFadden in Magheraclogher and they had two known children; Daniel (b. ~1858) and Maggie (b. ~1873). Henry Gallagher was dead by 1901 and in 1901 census his widowed wife Catherine, 60, resided with her son Daniel Gallagher, 43, a farmer in Magheraclogher, and his wife Ellen, 30, and his family. In 1911 census Catherine, 76, a widow, still resided at the same farm in Magheraclogher with her son Daniel, 53, and wife Ellen, 41, her grandchildren and her daughter Maggie.

Charlie's other paternal great-grandfather was Daniel Boyle and his great-grandmother was Sarah Doherty, aka Sally, both born around 1840 in Magheraclogher. Daniel Boyle married wife Sarah Doherty and they had a known daughter Ellen (b. 12 October 1867) in Magheraclogher.

Chapter 15

John Hughes (forward)

Honours as a Celtic player:

1 European Cup

6 Scottish League titles

1 Scottish Cup

4 Scottish League Cups

The young John Hughes

John Hughes, nicknamed 'Yogi' by his teammates, was born as day dawned on 3 April 1943 at 72 Barrowfield Street, Coatbridge, Lanarkshire to father James Hughes, a creamery despatch clerk, and mother Margaret Lennon. The birth was registered by John's father James later that same day at the Coatbridge Registry Office. At that time James and Margaret, married for just a year, were living at Bredisholm Road, Baillieston. John Hughes, age 16, was signed on provisional forms for Celtic from Shotts Bon Accord in 1959 and quickly established himself as a regular in the Hoops forward line. He was comfortable on both wings and in the centre forward position and could easily change positions during the course of a game with his versatility. He made his debut against Third Lanark on 13 August 1960 in a League Cup tie at Parkhead and scored in a 2-1 victory. John earned rave reviews when he scored twice in an impressive 4-0 win over Airdrie in the 1961 Scottish Cup semi-final.

Although the early 1960's were a painful time for Celtic due to the club's lack of success, big John's performances were one of the brighter spots. He was a fine goal scorer. The 1962-63 league championship was a good season for Yogi, nick-named after cartoon character Yogi Bear, even though he had a couple of periods out with a troublesome ankle injury. In the summer break in 1963 Celtic received a bid for Hughes from Italian side Juventus of Turin, however, this was turned down. In March 1964, John scored Celtic's winner in the notable 1-0 win over the Czech side Slovan Bratislava in the quarter finals of the European Cup Winners Cup. Hughes had a fine game in September 1964 against Rangers at Park-head on a mud heap of a pitch when he began to show that he was at last realising his great potential. In January 1965 he had an awesome game in the 8-0 win over Aberdeen on a very frosty Parkhead pitch, when John played in his 'sannies' and kept on his feet to tremendous effect, scoring a remarkable five goals in the process.

Life changed for everyone at Parkhead, including big Yogi, in March 1965 when Jock Stein arrived as manager. Hughes was the centre forward in the 1965 Scottish Cup final win against Dunfermline which started Celtic's greatest ever run. In October 1965 he showed remarkable coolness when scor-ing twice from the spot in the 2-1 League Cup final win over Rangers which showed that Celtic were now a real force back at the top of Scottish football. In May 1966 John won his first League medal but Celtic lost the Scottish Cup to Rangers in a replay. The 1966-67 season was never to be forgotten -

but John was to miss out in the European Cup final win in Lisbon due to injury. He played in five of the nine European games that season and John deserves to be remembered as a fully-fledged Lisbon Lion.

John's parents – James Hughes and Margaret Lennon

James Hughes was born on 10 March 1919 at 47 Main Street, Baillieston, Old Monkland to father John Hughes, an underground colliery fireman, and mother Margaret Corrins. The birth was registered by James's father John on 12 March 1919 at the Baillieston Registry Office. Two years later John's mother was born in Coatbridge, Lanarkshire. Margaret Lennon was born on 30 March 1921 at 35D Kirk-wood Street, Coatbridge to father William Lennon, a coal miner, and mother Annie Kane. The birth was registered by Margaret's father William on 4 April 1921 at the Coatbridge Registry Office. After they both left school, James got a job as a creamery despatch checker, most likely at what is now known as Cardowan Creameries, and Margaret got a job as a clothing factory machinist.

James Hughes, 25, a creamery despatch checker, residing at 112 Bredisholm Road, Baillieston married Margaret Lennon, 21, a clothing factory machinist, still residing at 35D Kirk-wood Street, Coatbridge on 7 April 1942 at St Augustine's Church, Coatbridge according to the forms of the Roman Catholic Church. The wedding was conducted by Father Edmund Macdonald, RC clergyman at St Augustine's; the witnesses were Henry and Elizabeth Hughes, James's brother and sister, both of 112 Bredisholm Road, Baillieston. Their son John Hughes was born on 3 April 1943 at 72 Barrowfield Street, Coatbridge. The birth was registered by John's father James later that same day at the Coatbridge Registry Office.

John's paternal grandparents – John Hughes and Margaret Corrins

John's paternal grandfather John Hughes was born around 1880 to father Terence Hughes, a coal miner, and mother Margaret McKinney. When John left school he followed his father down into the dark bowels of the Lanarkshire coalfields, probably at nearby Glenduffhill Colliery, Shettleston, and also became a coal miner. John's grandmother Margaret Corrins was born about 1883 to father John Corrins, also a coal miner, and mother Margaret Cougans. When Margaret left school she got a job as a pithead worker and it was probably at the pithead that she met her young sweetheart John Hughes.

John Hughes, 27, a coal miner, residing at 12 Sandyhill Square, Shettleston married Margaret Corrins, 24, a pithead worker, residing at 35 Muirside, Baillieston on 14 June 1907 at St Bridget's RC Church, Baillieston according to the forms of the Roman Catholic Church. The wedding was conducted by Father Peter H Terken, Catholic clergyman; the best man was Thomas Murray and the best maid was Ellen Corrins, Margaret's sister. Once again the observant reader will note that Father Peter H Terken had the privilege of marrying two other ancestors of a Lisbon Lions player. Father Peter also married Jimmy Johnstone's grandparents Matthew Johnstone and Theresa McDermott on 14 July 1899 at the RC Church, Baillieston.

John and Margaret had three known children; daughter Elizabeth, sons Henry and James. Their son James Hughes was born on 10 March 1919 at 47 Main Street, Baillieston. The birth was registered by James's father John Hughes on 12 March 1919 at the Baillieston Registry Office. During WWII, John Hughes, a colliery fireman, and his wife Margaret were both still alive and living in Baillieston.

John's maternal grandparents – William Lennon and Annie Kane

On John's maternal side, his grandfather William Lennon was born around 1883 to father Thomas Lennon, a tube work labourer, and mother Elizabeth McDougall. When William left school he was another of the Lions' ancestors to become a Lanarkshire coal miner. John's maternal grandmother Annie Kane was born around 1884 to father Patrick Kane, an iron work labourer, and mother Mary McQuiggan. After her schooling Annie went into domestic service like many young girls in the Victorian era.

William Lennon, 22, a coal miner, residing at 59 Coatbank Street, Coatbridge married wife Annie Kane, 21, a domestic servant, on 13 July 1905 at St Patrick's Church, Coatbridge according to the forms of the Roman Catholic Church. The wedding was conducted by Father R Canavan, RC clergyman; the witnesses were Patrick and Mary Kane, likely to be

Annie's brother and sister. Their daughter Margaret Lennon was born on 30 March 1921 at 35D Kirkwood Street, Coatbridge. The birth was registered by Margaret's father William on 4 April 1921 at the Coatbridge Registry Office. During WWII, William was a widowed tube work labourer in Coatbridge. His wife Annie was dead by then.

John's great-grandparents

Like many of the other players John's great-grandparents were all born around the mid-19th century and again most likely to be of Irish heritage. John's paternal great-grandfather was Terence Hughes, a coal miner, and his great-grandmother was Margaret McKinney and they had a son John (b. ~1880). Terence and Margaret were both dead by 1907 when their son John married in Baillieston. Still on the paternal side his other great-grandfather was John Corrins, also a coal miner, and his great-grandmother was Margaret Cougans. John and Margaret had two known daughters; Margaret (b. ~1883) and Ellen. John Corrins, a coal miner, and wife Margaret were still alive in 1907 when their daughter Margaret married John Hughes in Baillieston.

On John's maternal side his great-grandfather was Thomas Lennon, a tube work labourer, and his great-grandmother was Elizabeth McDougall and they had a son William (b. ~1883). Thomas and Elizabeth were still alive in 1905 when son William married in 1905 in Coatbridge. John's other maternal great-grandfather was Patrick Kane, an iron work labourer, and his great-grandmother was Mary McQuiggan.

Patrick and Mary had three known children; son Patrick and daughters Annie (b. ~1884) and Mary. Patrick Kane, an iron work labourer, and his wife Mary were both dead by 1905, when their daughter Annie married William Lennon in Coatbridge.

Chapter 16

Willie O'Neill (full-back)

Honours as a Celtic player:
1 European Cup
1 Scottish League Cup

The young Willie O'Neill

William O'Neill was born on 30 December 1940 at 165 Springfield Road, Shettleston, Glasgow to father William O'Neill, a tramcar conductor, and mother Frances Patrick. The birth was registered by Willie's father William on Hogmanay, 31 December 1940, at the Glasgow Registry Office. He joined Celtic from St Anthony's in October 1959 and went on to spend the best part of the next decade at Parkhead. Willie made his Hoops first team debut at left back in the Scottish Cup final replay of 1961, as the Celts lost 2-0 to Dunfermline at Hampden Park, replacing defender Jim Kennedy who had been sent to hospital with appendicitis.

Willie was a precision passer and kept a cool head, but for most of his Celtic career he had to be content with infrequent first team call ups, due to stiff competition from Duncan

McKay, Tommy Gemmell, Iain Young and more especially Jim Craig. However, at the start of the now legendary 1966-67 season, Stein gave Willie his chance and he turned in some fine performances most notably against Rangers in the League Cup final of October 1966. With Celtic leading 1-0 and under severe pressure with only minutes remaining, the Gers forward Alec Smith prodded the ball past Ronnie Simpson towards the Celtic goal but Willie saved the day by clearing the ball off the goal line.

Willie played in the first four European ties of the 1966-67 season, which qualified him for his winner's medal, but despite some fine performances he was dropped by Stein after the disappointing 3-2 Hogmanay defeat to Dundee United. Willie was one of the more traditional defensively-minded full-backs and he tended to remain back in his own half most of the time and rarely ventured forward. Stein was beginning to mould Jim Craig and Tommy Gemmell into modern overlapping attacking full-backs. In the New Year of 1967, Jim Craig took Willie's place and the young dental student never looked back. However, Stein did recall Willie to play in Alfredo di Stefano's testimonial in the Bernabeau stadium against the legendary Real Madrid and he excelled in Celtic's historic 1-0 victory.

Willie's parents – William O'Neill and Frances Patrick
Willie's father William O'Neill was born on 15 February 1904 at 21 Rumford Street, Bridgeton, Glasgow to father John O'Neill, an oil refiner, and mother Elizabeth McEwan.

The birth was registered by Willie's mother Elizabeth on 5 March 1904 at the Glasgow Registry Office. It might surprise most Celtic fans to know that Willie's mother Frances Patrick was actually born as Fransziki Ziamaytis (aka Francjida or Francesca) on 26 November 1909 at 508 Baltic Street, Bridgeton to Polish-born immigrants, and her father was Anthony Ziamaytis, a coal miner, and mother Anna Babarskinta. The birth was registered by Frances's father Anthony, who signed with his 'x' mark, on 4 December 1909 at the Glasgow Registry Office.

In 1911 census Francesca Ziamitis, age 1, still resided at 508 Baltic Street, Bridgeton with her parents Anthony and Annie, her sister Mary and four young Polish-born boarders. In the early half of the 20th century Baltic Street in Dalmarnock gave its name to one of the many notorious Glasgow razor gangs, the Catholic Baltic Fleet, whose sworn enemies were the Protestant Brigton Billy Boys. Bridgeton, and indeed Glasgow, in the 1920s and 30s had a proliferation of gangs generally split along sectarian lines and the area also boasted the Norman Conks, from Norman Street, and the Brigton Derry Boys.

The author is reminded of an amusing tale that his late mother-in-law Jean Downie related when she was a very young girl in the late 1940s and living in the Protestant enclave of 'little' Norman Street, Bridgeton with her widowed mother Jeanie. Jeanie had decided one evening to send Jean out to get fish suppers for their tea, but Jeanie had espied from her tenement window that the Norman Conks were battling against one of their Protestant enemies down at the Catholic end of 'big' Norman Street.

The best chip shop was Jimmy's on 'big' Norman Street, but Jeanie, who was a very strict mother, warned Jean not to go to Jimmy's. She ordered her daughter to go around the corner to the chip shop on French Street, which was not as good quality. Of course, the tiny Jean disobeyed her mother and marched confidently through the battling gangs on Norman Street. Jean remembered that all the men and boys actually stopped fighting to let her pass on to the chip shop on Norman Street. In those violent times, what gang members did to each other was horrendous, but they had a code of chivalry and a female would not be touched. While Jean and Jeanie sat eating their fish and chips, Jeanie, detecting the better taste, looked up and exclaimed angrily, "You went to Jimmy's, didn't you?"

William O'Neill must have been very familiar with many of those Bridgeton gang members for by 1935 he was living in Reid Street, Bridgeton, and working as a prison warder, almost certainly at Glasgow's notorious east end Barlinnie Prison. Around this time William met and fell in love with Frances Patrick, a lappet weaver, who was living at nearby Poplin Street. **Lappet** weaving is defined as a type of weaving into which an embroidered pattern produced by additional warp threads has been introduced with the aid of a **lappet** tool.

William O'Neill, 31, a prison warder, residing at 128 Reid Street, Bridgeton married Frances Patrick (formerly known as Francjida Ziamaytis), 28, a lappet weaver, residing at 43 Poplin Street, Bridgeton on 11 July 1935 at Sacred Heart Church, Bridgeton according to the forms of the Roman Catholic Church. The wedding was conducted by Father Anthony Mullins, priest at Sacred Heart; the witnesses were Peter and Ellen Patrick, Frances's brother and sister.

By the start of WWII, William had packed in his job as a prison warder at the 'Bar-L' and he had started working as a tramcar conductor, almost certainly at Dalmarnock Tramway Depot in Ruby Street, Bridgeton where the author's mother-in-law Jean's father - Harry Downie – also worked as a tramcar driver, until he died in 1941.

The start of the war probably gave William his chance to get out of his stressful job at Barlinnie. With all the young Glasgow gangsters preferring to go off and have a scrap with the Nazis instead of each other, the prisons would not be quite as full. With many young men away fighting there would certainly be vacancies to fill at Dalmarnock Tramway Depot. William and Frances's son William O'Neill was born on 30 December 1940 at 165 Springfield Road, Shettleston. The birth was registered by Willie's father William on Hogmanay, 31 December 1940, at the Glasgow Registry Office.

Willie's paternal grandparents – John O'Neill and Elizabeth McEwan

Willie's paternal grandfather John O'Neill was born around 1869 to father also John O'Neill, a labourer, and mother Jane Hacket. By 1898 John was working as an oil refiner, almost certainly at the Rumford Street Chemical Works. George Miller & Company's Rumford Street Chemical Works was constructed on a site adjoining the City & Suburban Gas Company's Dalmarnock Gas Works; both of which began production around 1844. The chemical works processed the by-products of gas production, and supplied tars and asphalt from their 'Dalmarnock Asphalt Works', used for flooring and pavement works.

From 1866 to 1872 the Glasgow Post Office directories listed George Miller & Co. under 'Paraffin Oil Manufacturers', suggesting that shale oil may have been refined at Rumford Street during this period of 'oil mania'. The works were last listed in the 1905 Glasgow Post Office Directory as follows:-

> *Miller, George, & Co., gas coal-tar distillers, manufacturers of sulphate of ammonia, napthas, benzoles, pitch, carbolic acid, creosote, and dipping oils, 40 West Nile Street; works, 89 Rumford Street.*

It may have been whilst walking up and down Rumford Street that John O'Neill met and fell in love with paper mill worker Elizabeth McEwan, as the song from My Fair Lady goes, 'there, on the street where she lives'. Willie's paternal grandmother Elizabeth McEwan was also born around 1869 to father Robert McEwan, an engine fitter, and mother Elizabeth McCann. John O'Neill, who was almost certainly Catholic, and Elizabeth McEwan, a Protestant, had what is known in Glasgow as a 'mixed marriage'. John and Elizabeth were married in a civil ceremony in 1898, which was unusual in the Victorian era, although the book has already described a similar civil marriage for two of Bertie Auld's ancestors. John O'Neill, 29, an oil refiner, residing at 231 Main Street, Bridgeton married Elizabeth McEwan, 29, a paper mill worker, residing at 21 Rumford Street, Bridgeton on 11 November 1898, by warrant of the Sheriff Substitute for Lanarkshire. The wedding was held at 216 Dalmarnock

Road, Glasgow; the witnesses were William Skinner, a clerk, and his wife Margaret Skinner, nee Farrell, both of 7 Kirk Street, Calton.

Son William O'Neill was born on 15 February 1904 at 21 Rumford Street, Bridgeton. The birth was registered by Willie's mother Elizabeth on 5 March 1904 at the Glasgow Registry Office. It appears that just over a year later the Rumford Street Chemical Works was closed down. John later became an engineer's slinger, employed to transfer engineering goods from wagons using a sling. John O'Neill, an engineer's slinger, and his wife Elizabeth were still alive in 1935 and living in Bridgeton.

Willie's maternal grandparents – Anthony Ziamaytis and Anna Babarskinta

On Willie's maternal side his grandfather Anthony Ziamaytis (or Ziamitis) was born around 1871 and his wife Anna Babarskinta, aka Annie, was born around 1872 both in Eastern Poland, which at that time was part of the Tzarist Russian Empire. Throughout the 19th century Poland's geopolitical location on the Northern European Lowlands became especially important in a period when its expansionist neighbours, the Kingdom of Prussia, which ruled Silesia and Western Poland, and their great enemies Imperialist Russia which ruled over the Eastern Poland-Lithuanian Commonwealth, involved themselves intensely in European rivalries and alliances. This rivalry intensified about the time of Anthony and Anna's births when Chancellor Otto von Bismarck created the new unified Germany in 1871.

The new German Reich aimed at the assimilation of its eastern provinces inhabited by Poles. At the same time, St. Petersburg attempted to make the former Congress of Poland more Russian. The Tsar joined Berlin in levying restrictions against the use of the Polish language and cultural expression. Poles under Russian and German rule also endured official campaigns against the Roman Catholic Church. The Cultural Struggle (Kulturkampf) was instigated by Bismarck to bring the Roman Catholic Church under state control and the Tsar campaigned to extend Russian Orthodoxy throughout the empire. Millions of Poles, mainly Catholics and political emigres, fled to the USA, Britain and Western Europe to escape religious and cultural persecution.

Anthony Ziamaytis married Anna Babarskinta around 1903, probably while still living in Eastern Poland, and they immigrated to Bridgeton, Glasgow a couple of years later. In Bridgeton, they had three known daughters Mary (b. ~1908), Frances (b. 1909), Ellen and a son Peter. Their daughter Fransziki Ziamaytis (aka Francjida or Francesca) was born on 26 November 1909 at 508 Baltic Street, Bridgeton. The birth was registered by Frances's father Anthony, who signed with his 'x' mark, on 4 December 1909 at the Glasgow Registry Office.

In 1911 census Anthony Ziamitas, 30, a coal miner hewer, still resided at 508 Baltic Street, Bridgeton with wife Annie, 29, and daughters Mary, 3, and baby Francesca, 1. Also boarding at Anthony's home were four other Russian-Polish born lodgers, all also working as coal miner hewers; Joseph Patrick, 26, Andrew Dollo, 52, George Rowarskis, 21, and Joseph Karpavitch. It is significant that a Pole named Joseph

Patrick was staying with Anthony and he may even have been Anthony's brother, who had already decided to anglicize his name, because it appears that the Ziamaytis family later changed their surname to Patrick. Anthony Ziamaytis, a coal miner, was dead by 1935, and his wife Anna Babarskinta was a widow, when their daughter Frances Patrick married husband William O'Neill.

Willie's great-grandparents

Only Willie's paternal great-grandparents have been identified and they were also born around the mid-19th century and some, if not all, are certainly to be of Irish descent. Willie's paternal great-grandfather was John O'Neill, a labourer, and his great-grandmother was Jane Hacket and they had a son John (b. ~1869). John, a labourer, and Jane were both dead by 1898, when their son John married in Bridgeton, Glasgow.

Still on the paternal side, his other great-grandfather was Robert McEwan, an engine fitter, and his great-grandmother was Elizabeth McCann. Robert and Elizabeth had a daughter Elizabeth (b. ~1869). Robert McEwan, an engine fitter, was dead by 1898 and his wife Elizabeth was a widow at that date, when their daughter Elizabeth married John O'Neill in Bridgeton.

Conclusion

First and foremost, this book is a celebration of the achievement of a group of young Scottish lads who, 50 years ago
on 25 May 1967, achieved the extraordinary feat of winning
the European Cup. Never again in the annals of football are
we likely to see a team with players of humble backgrounds,
all born within thirty miles of their local club, like Celtic,
march on to win club football's most prized trophy.

The family histories of the players wholly underlines the
humbleness of their ancestral origins. These were men and
women who criss-crossed Scotland to scratch a meagre living
as agricultural labourers, coal miners, shipyard workers, jute
weavers and domestic servants throughout the Dickensian
Victorian era. Poverty-stricken people who emigrated from
Ireland to escape famine and destitution in the mid-19th
century; who fled from Eastern Europe in the late 19th
century to escape the rise of Prussian Imperialism, Tsarist
domination and religious persecution.

Into the 20th century the family histories tell of the struggle to survive during two devastating World Wars and the
desperate poverty during the Great Depression of the 1930s.
In many ways the family histories of these men and women
are no different to our own family histories. Most of us can
trace our ancestry back to humble beginnings throughout the
Agrarian and Industrial Revolutions. What defines this book

is the culmination of these specific family histories in producing 16 remarkable young 'Bhoys' who went on to create what was arguably the greatest Scottish sporting achievement of the 20th century.

In conclusion, this book celebrates – the Lisbon Lions.

Player References

Sure it's a Grand Old Team to Play For, Ronnie Simpson, 1967

Jim Craig: A Lion Looks Back, Jim Craig, 1998

Tommy Gemmell: Lion Heart, Tommy Gemmell with Graham McColl, 2012

All the way with Celtic, Bobby Murdoch, 1970

Hail Cesar: An Autobiography, Billy McNeill, 2004

Fire in my Boots, Jimmy Johnstone, 1969

Heart of a Lion: The life and times of Lisbon Lion, William Wallace, 2013

Stevie Chalmers: The Winning Touch, Stevie Chalmers with Graham McColl, 2012

A Bhoy called Bertie, Bertie Auld and Alex Gordon, 2008

Thirty Miles from Paradise, Bobby Lennox, 2008

John Fallon: Keeping in Paradise, John Fallon and David Potter, 2015

Charlie Gallacher: What a Player, David Potter, 2016

Yogi Bare: The Life and Times of Celtic legend John Hughes, John Hughes and Alex Gordon, 2014

Genealogical References

Statutory Registrations of Births, Marriages and Deaths, Census Records and Old Parish Registers: National Records of Scotland, General Register House, Edinburgh

1901 and 1911 censuses: National Archives of Ireland, census. nationalarchives.ie

Lindel Buckley, Donegal Genealogy Resources

Association of Scottish Genealogists and Researchers in Archives (ASGRA)

Online and Other References

The Mitchell Library

National Library of Scotland (digital.nls.uk/directories)

ScotlandsPlaces.gov.uk

The Glasgow Herald

The Scotsman

The Daily Telegraph

Oxford Dictionary of National Biography

Dictionary.com

Wikipedia.co.uk

The Celtic Wiki

The Glasgow Story

Royston Road Project

Surname Database

Ayrshire Roots

ThreeTowners.net

Scottishmining.co.uk

Scottishshale.co.uk

FootlightNotes.tumblr.com: Sir Harry Lauder

YouTube: John McCormick

Paddy Whacked, The untold story of the Irish American Gangster,
T J English, 2006

Glossary of Players' Origin of Surnames

Part 1:

Chapter 1: Simpson – a surname of Anglo-Scottish origin generally believed to be derived from 'the son of Simon'

Chapter 2: Craig – a Scottish locational surname derived from the Gaelic 'creag' meaning a rock

Chapter 3: Gemmell – a surname of Old Norse or Viking origin from the personal byname 'Gamall' meaning 'the old one'.

Chapter 4: Murdoch – a surname of Gaelic origin originally 'muiredach' meaning 'belonging to the sea', in other words, a mariner.

Chapter 5: McNeill – a Scottish surname of Gaelic origin, although also common in Antrim and Derry, meaning 'the son of Neil'. Neil is an ancient personal name most likely of Olde Norse origin 'njal' and in Gaelic 'niadh' meaning champion. (See also O'Neill below)

Chapter 6: Clark – a long established surname of Anglo-Saxon origin, which effectively was occupational for a secretary or scribe, however, as in olden days the only people who could write were usually of religious orders, which derives from the Olde English 'clerc' meaning a priest and the modern word cleric also derives from the same origin.

Chapter 7: Johnstone – a Scottish locational surname believed to derive from the Norman held lands of Johnstone in Dumfriesshire, the original overlord granted lands there was named Jonis and thus the homesteading became known as 'Jonis toun'.

Chapter 8: Wallace – after Bruce is this the most famous Scottish surname? It is actually believed to be an old Brittonic surname derived from the Norman French word 'waleis' meaning foreigner, which the Normans applied to the Welsh, Celts and Britons. The Celtic inhabitants from Hadrian's Wall to the Clyde Valley, where Sir William Wallace was born, were known as the 'walensis'.

Chapter 9: Chalmers – a Scottish variant of the English surname Chambers and effectively an occupational surname for an officer in charge of a lord's private living quarters or chambers, also known as a chamberlain.

Chapter 10: Auld – an Anglo-Saxon surname derived from the Olde English 'eald' simply meaning old, but probably began as nickname to distinguish an elder from a younger person with the same forename.

Chapter 11: Lennox – a famous Scottish surname derived from the lands of the Lennox in Dunbartonshire but derives from the Gaelic 'leamhanach' and later written as Levenaux meaning 'one belonging to the elm field'.

Part 2:

Chapter 12: Fallon – an Anglicized surname of Irish Gaelic origin from O'Fallaimhan and meaning 'son of Fallamhan' who would have been a chieftain, taken from 'follamhnas' meaning supremacy.

Chapter 13: McBride – another Anglicized surname of Irish Gaelic origin from 'mac giolla Brighde' meaning 'son of the servant of St Bridget' usually meaning St Brigid of Kildare.

Chapter 14: Gallagher – an ancient Irish Gaelic surname derived from the Irish Gaelic 'O'Gallchobair' and is believed to be a compound of 'gall' meaning foreign and 'cabhair' meaning helper, thus the Gallaghers may originally have been foreign mercenaries and are particular to County Donegal. The O'Gallaghers are said to be descended from the Cineal Connaill line, one of the families descended from Connall Gulban, son of Niall of the Nine Hostages.

Chapter 15: Hughes – originally an Olde French personal name in Ireland and Scotland it became in Gaelic 'aodh' meaning 'fire' in the sense of one who is full of fire or an inspired one.

Chapter 16: O'Neill – like McNeill above instead this is an Irish surname variant of Gaelic origin, meaning 'the son of Neil' and from the Gaelic 'niadh' meaning 'champion'. The O'Neills claim descent from Niall Glundubh (Neil the Black Knee), the legendary King of Ireland also known as Niall of the Nine Hostages. There were two main branches of the O'Neill lines, the southern branch was mostly associated with County Meath. The northern branch of the O'Neills were the more famous line and had extensive lands in Ulster and who became the 'Earls of Tyrone'. Dare it be stated in this book? The Red Hand of Ulster was taken from the coat of arms of the O'Neills of Ulster!

Glossary of Key Names (excludes Jock Stein and the Lions as they are widely discussed)

Chapter 1: Ronnie Simpson

Batchelor, Thomas

Baxter, Jim

Brown, Bobby

Busby, Matt

Campbell, Alexandra

Campbell, James M, Rev.

Campbell, Mabel Norma Samson

Campbell, Robert Clark

Davidson, Janet

Davidson, Mary R

Dick, David, Rev.

Giffen, John

Greig, Jean

Henderson, Euphemia

Henderson, Mary

Hodge, Lindsay

Hodge, Mr, Headmaster

Howatson, Annie McMillan

Howatson, Polly

Howatson, William

Hunter, Jane

Kerr, Robert Taggart, Rev.

Law, Denis

McCracken, Grace

McGee, Archie

McGonagall, William Topaz

Glossary of Key Names cont'd

Robertson, Elizabeth Imrie

Robertson, William

Samson, Lily

Shaw, Alex

Simpson, Agnes

Simpson, Alexander

Simpson, Elizabeth

Simpson, Elspet

Simpson, James

Simpson, James Annan

Simpson, James McMillan

Simpson, Jean

Simpson, John

Simpson, R A

Simpson, Robert

Simpson, Ronald Campbell

Chapter 2: Jim Craig

Burns, Bartholomew, Fr.

Busby, Matt, Sir

Craig, James Philip

Craig, James Forbes McIntyre

Craig, James Forbes McIntyre (Sr)

Craig, John

Craig, John Nelson

Craig, Mary

Craig, William

Ferdinand, Franz, Archduke

Ferguson, Alex, Sir

Flynn, Margaret

Foreman, Ann

Foreman, David

Foreman, Lillias

Foreman, Margaret

Foreman, Thomas

Foreman, Thomas (Sr)

Foreman, William

Hughes, Anna

Hughes, John

Hughes, Margaret

Hughes, Patrick

Hughes, Philip

Hughes, Philip (Sr)

Innes, Annie

Lindsay, Harriet

McBrearty, G, Fr.

McGrory, Jimmy

Princip, Gavrilo

Reid, Alexander

Richardson, Charles, Rev.

Shankly, Bill

Welsh, Elizabeth

Wisdom, Annie Bridget

Wisdom, Mary Ellen

Wisdom, Thomas

Wright, Jane

Young, Iain

<u>Glossary of Key Key Names cont'd</u>

Chapter 3: Tommy Gemmell

Buchan, Thomas, Rev.

Closs, Charles

Collie, Annie

Coyle, M, Fr.

Gemmell, Alfred

Gemmell, Henry

Gemmell, Thomas

Gemmell, Thomas (Jr)

Gemmell, Thomas (Sr)

Gemmell, Winifred

Gorman, James

Gorman, Joseph

Gorman, Joseph (Sr)

Gorman, Lizzie Jane

Gorman, Maggie

Gorman, Mary

Gorman, William

Hamilton, Alexander

Hamilton, Catherine Benbeth

Hamilton, David

Hamilton, David (Sr)

Hamilton, Elizabeth Stewart

Hamilton, Janet

Hamilton, John

Hamilton, Robert

Houston, Agnes

Johnstone, Anna

McGrory, Jimmy

Queen, John

Richards, Charles

Robertson, Annie

Smellie, Janet

Stewart, Ann

Stewart, Archibald

Stewart, David

Stewart, Elizabeth

Stewart, George

Stewart, John

Stewart, Margaret Miller

Stewart, William

Todd, Anna

Todd, Francis

Chapter 4: Bobby Murdoch

Clark, John, AFM Freight, Motherwell

Hart, Barbara

Hitler, Adolf

Kelly, John

Kelly, Mary

Kerr, James

Lavery, David

Lynch, Andrew, Fr.

MacDonald, Barbara

MacDonald, James

MacDonald, William

McGory, Mary

McLean, Elizabeth Fisher

Moran, Mary Ann

Mullins, Anthony, Fr.

Glossary of Key Names cont'd

Murdoch, Donald

Murdoch, Edward

Murdoch, George

Murdoch, John

Murdoch, John McDonald

Murdoch, Matthew Watson

Murdoch, Mary

Murdoch, Robert White

Murdoch, Robert White (Sr)

Murdoch, William

Shades, Mary

Souness, Graeme

Sweeney, Mary

Vallance, William, Rev.

White, Mary Jane

White, Robert

White, Robert (Sr)

White, Rose Ann

White, Sarah

Chapter 5: Billy McNeill

Basanavicius, Jonas

Bonnett, James, Pte.

Bungard, Stanley

Collins, Bobby

Evans, Bobby

Haughney, Mike

Jerbulei, Agata

Jurkeniute, Anton

Jurkeniute, Urzula

Kelly, Robert, Sir

Latikavicz, Marie

McArthur, Jane

McArthur, Margaret

McCardle, Eddie

McCue, Margaret

McNeill, Francis Lindsay

McNeill, Henry (or McArthur)

McNeill, James

McNeill, James (Sr)

McNeill, William

McNeill, William (Sr)

McNeill, Williamina (or Glenday)

Mitchell, Ellen

Mitchell, Grace

Mitchell, Thomas

Power, Les, Fr.

Tully, Charlie

Walatkeviczus, Alene

Walatkeviczus, Grazia

Walatkeviczus, Kazis

Walatkeviczus, Mikelaitu

Chapter 6: John Clark

Clark, Catherine

Clark, Helen

Clark, James

Clark, James (Sr)

Clark, John Patrick

Clark, John

Clark, John (Sr)

Glossary of Key Names cont'd

Clark, Mary

Clark, Owen

Clark, Roseann

Clark, Sarah

Coughlan, Bridget

Doyle, Elizabeth

Doyle, Michael

Everett, Ann

Gilmour, Elizabeth

McGowan, Ellen

Peacock, Bertie

Rourke, Thomas, Fr.

Smith, Bridget

Smith, Bernard

Smith, James

Smith, Margaret

Stiphout, Stubart van, Fr.

Chapter 7: Jimmy Johnstone

Busby, Matt, Sir

Cairney, Frank

Crawley, Patrick

Crawley, Sarah

Crines, John

Dalglish, Kenny

Devlin, Catherine

Dougan, James

Greer, Mary

Gribben, Jimmy

Hartie, Mary

Chapter 8: Willie Wallace

Glossary of Key Names cont'd

Brown, William Semple

Cumming, Lauchlan

Glen, Catherine

Glen, Hugh

Glen, Jane

Irvine, David

Mackie, James, Rev.

Maxwells of Pollok

McBlane, Mary

McCue, Thomas

McLellan, James

McLellan, Margaret

McLellan, Sarah White

Morrison, J Angus, Rev.

Semple, Janet

Stirling, Agnes

Stirling-Maxwell of Pollok

Tonner, Mary (aka Marian)

Wallace, Andrew

Wallace, Andrew (Jr)

Wallace, Andrew (Sr)

Wallace, Hugh

Wallace, James

Wallace, Maggie

Wallace, William Semple Brown

Chapter 9: Stevie Chalmers
Chalmers, Catherine

Chalmers, David

Chalmers, David (Jr)

Chalmers, David (Sr)

Chalmers, Elizabeth

Chalmers, Isabella

Chalmers, James

Chalmers, John

Chalmers, Thomas

Chalmers, Thomas Stephen

Chalmers, William

Conway, Elizabeth

Danaher, James, Fr.

Hand, James

Hetherington, Robert

Hunter, Mary Love

Hunter, William

Kelly, Charles J

McAvoy, William, Fr.

MacGregor, Rob Roy

McGrory, Jimmy

McLaren, Eliza

Murphy, Catherine

Murray, Elizabeth

Nevans, Agnes

Nevans, John

Nevans, Joseph

Nevans, Margaret (or Nevins)

Nevans, Mary

Nevans, Michael

Nevans, Teresa

Nevans, Thomas

Nevans, Thomas (Sr)

<u>Glossary of Key Names cont'd</u>

Nevans, William

Thomson, E L, Rev.

Trainer, Agnes

Welsh, Jane

Wood, Margaret Campbell
Chapter 10: Robert Auld

Auld, Allan

Auld, John Lambie

Auld, Robert

Auld, Robert (Sr)

Blest, Bernard

Boyd, Matilda

Burns, Robert

Devlin, Anna

Devlin, Helen

Devlin, Henry

Devlin, Hugh

Devlin, James

Devlin, John

Devlin, Margaret

Devlin, Margaret Diamond

Devlin, Thomas

Diamond, Margaret

Douglas, William, Captain

Halliday, A B, Rev.

Halliday, the butcher

Hannay, John, Rev.

Lauder, Harry, Sir

Laurie, Annie

Lockhart, John

McCormack, John

McCrae, James

McCrae, Wilhelmina

McGrory, Jimmy

McNellis, John

Montgomery, Marion

Rogers, Elizabeth

Scott, John, Lady

Semple, William

Stewart, Archibald

Stewart, Elizabeth

Ward, Martin

Chapter 11: Bobby Lennox

Clark, George Caie

Collie, Annie

Collins, Bobby

Dillon, Isabella

Dillon, James

Dillon, Jeanie

Duggan, Margaret

Erskine, Agnes Murphit Murray Dillon

Erskine, Annie

Erskine, Patrick

Erskine, Patrick (Sr)

Evans, Bobby

Guthrie, Susan

Harris, Robert

Harris, Susan

Keogh, William, Fr.

Glossary of Key Names cont'd

Lennox, Andrew

Lennox, Patrick

Lennox, Robert

Lennox, Robert (Sr)

Lynch, Hugh

McAvoy, Annie

McGrory, Jimmy

MacKintosh, James, Fr.

McQuade, Arthur

Mochan, Neil

Murphy, Agnes

Murray, Agnes

Nicol. Andrew

Nobel, Alfred

Peacock, Bertie

Rooney, John, Fr.

Tully, Charlie

Chapter 12: John Fallon

Callaghan, Mary

Cassidy, Elizabeth

Devine, Bernard

Docherty, Tommy

Doyle, James Joseph, Fr.

Fallon, John James

Fallon, Lizzie

Fallon, Margaret

Fallon, Patrick

Fallon, Patrick (Jr)

Fallon, Patrick (Sr)

Fallon, Thomas

Galbraith, George, Fr.

Haffey, Frank

Keenan, Edward

Kelly, James CSC

Kelly, Jane

Lang, Mary

Loughrie, Maggie

Mentinsere, Louis de, Fr.

Murphy, Catherine

Murphy, John

Murray, Jane

Murray, Michael

Murray, Sarah

Murray, William

Sherry, Daniel

Sherry, Helen

Sime, Agnes

Chapter 13: Joe McBride

Cranston, Miss

Doyle, Thomas, Fr.

Feechan, Maggie

Ferguson, Alex, Sir

Gallagher, Catherine

Glen, Allan

Harkins, Mary

Harle, William

Honeyman, John

McBrearty, G, Fr.

McBride, Alexander

McBride, James

McBride, Joseph

McBride, Neil

McCormick, Catherine

McGowan, Beatrice

McGowan, Bridget

McGowan, Jean

McGowan, Michael

McGowan, Michael (Sr) re Michael

McGowan, Michael (Sr) re Bridget

McGowan, William

McGrory, Jimmy

Mackintosh, Charles Rennie

Neil, Mary

O'Neill, Catherine

O'Neill, Joseph

O'Neill, Martha

Sheehy, John J, Fr.

Thatcher, Margaret

Watt, Robert

Chapter 14: Charlie Gallagher

Best, George

Billingsly, Sherman

Boyle, Daniel

Boyle, Ellen

Charlton, Bobby, Sir

Coll, Peter

Coll, Rose

Coll, Toal

Coll, Vincent 'Mad Dog'

Crerand, Paddy

Doherty, Sarah

Duffy, Anne

Duffy, Charles

Duncan, Annie

Gallagher, Bridget aka Biddy

Gallagher, Catherine aka Kate

Gallagher, Charles

Gallagher, Charles James

Gallagher, Daniel

Gallagher, Daniel (Sr)

Gallagher, Doalty

Gallagher, Henry

Gallagher, Henry (Sr)

Gallagher, Maggie

Gallagher, Margaret

Gallagher, Mary

Gallagher, Patrick

Gallagher, Sarah

Gallagher, John aka Shane

Harkin, Rose

Kreisberger, Lottie

Law, Denis

Madden, Owney

Mange, George 'Big Frenchy' de

Mary, Queen of Scots

McCue, Margaret

McFadden, Catherine

McGarvey, Bridget

McGrory, Jimmy

Glossary of Key Names cont'd

Peoples, Michael

Schultz, Dutch

Stewarts of Castlemilk

Vallee, Rudi

Chapter 15: John Hughes

Canavan, R, Fr.

Corrins, Ellen

Corrins, John

Corrins, Margaret

Cougans, Margaret

Hughes, Elizabeth

Hughes, Henry

Hughes, James

Hughes, John

Hughes, John (Sr)

Hughes, Terence

Kane, Annie

Kane, Mary

Kane, Patrick

Kane, Patrick (Sr)

Lennon, Margaret

Lennon, Thomas

Lennon, William

Macdonald, Edmund, Fr.

McDougall, Elizabeth

McKinney, Margaret

McQuiggan, Mary

Murray, Thomas

Terken, Peter H, Fr.

Chapter 16: Willie O'Neill

Babarskinta, Anna

Bismarck, Otto von, Chancellor

Dollo, Andrew

Downie, Harry

Downie, Jean

Downie, Jeanie

Farrell, Margaret (or Skinner)

Hacket, Jane

Karpavitch, Joseph

Kennedy, Jim

McCann, Elizabeth

McEwan, Elizabeth

McEwan, Robert

McKay, Duncan

Mullins, Anthony, Fr.

O'Neill, John

O'Neill, John (Sr)

O'Neill, William

O'Neill, William (Sr)

Patrick, Ellen

Patrick, Frances

Patrick, Joseph

Patrick, Peter

Rowarskis, George

Skinner, William

Smith, Alec

Young, Iain

Ziamaytis, Anthony

Ziamaytis, Fransziki (or Francjida)

Ziamaytis, Mary

About the author

Derek Niven is a pseudonym used by the author John McGee, a member of ASGRA, in the publication of his factual and genealogical writings and Derek Beaugarde for his fictional science fiction writings. John McGee was born in 1956 in the railway village of Corkerhill, Glasgow and he attended Mosspark Primary and Allan Glen's schools. To explain; the late great actor Sir Derek Bogarde spent two unhappy years at Allan Glen's when he was a pupil named Derek Niven van den Bogaerde, thus the observant reader will readily be able to discern the origin of the two pseudonyms. After spending 34 years in the rail industry in train planning and accountancy John McGee retired in 2007. In 2012 the idea for his science fiction novel first emerged and 2084: The End of Days © Derek Beaugarde was published by Corkerhill Press in 2016. In the years leading up to 2084 seven disparate men and women across the globe find themselves battling with their own personal frailties and human tragedies. Suddenly they find themselves drawn together in order to fight for survival against the ultimate global disaster – Armageddon! 2084: The End of Days is their story and mankind's destiny. 2084 is available for purchase on Amazon.

By the same author

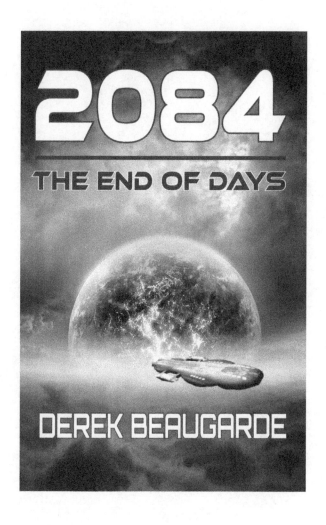

Printed in February 2022
by Rotomail Italia S.p.A., Vignate (MI) - Italy